Jeremy –
I hope you Enjoy my
memoir!
– Drew Paige –

THE
DARK
WIT

THE DARKNESS WITHIN

A MEMOIR

DREW PAIGE

NEW DEGREE PRESS

THE DARKNESS WITHIN

a memoir

ISBN   978-1-63676-440-5 *Paperback*

978-1-63676-441-2 *Kindle Ebook*

978-1-63676-442-9 *Ebook*

CONTENTS

———

AUTHOR'S NOTE

When we are brought into this world, no one tells us how difficult life is. It is like when you are getting married, not one person at the wedding says, "Hey, this shit is going to be really hard. Good luck!" Nope, they congratulate you, ask when you are planning a family, tell you to "enjoy the honeymoon"! That is how I look at my life. It has been a journey and not one person has told me how to navigate it. I have had to figure out life on my own.

After forty-four years, I felt it was my time to share my experiences with mental illness. I wanted to share the trials and tribulations I have experienced navigating life with a diagnosis of Bipolar two Disorder. From my own life journey, I want others who have family members with mental illness, or they themselves have a mental illness, to feel "normal," not stigmatized by what society says mental illness is.

Discrimination occurs when people talk about mental illness. Many people believe that people who are mentally ill are dangerous or crazy when in fact people who have a mental illness, including me, are just like everyone else. People who have mental illnesses also have steady jobs and function in society just the same as other people do. They have ongoing and lasting, loving relationships. The only difference is that people who have a mental illness have symptoms they have to manage daily. With the right treatment team, having a functioning great life is possible.

I was physically, verbally, and emotionally abused as well as covertly sexualized by my father. In response to the trauma of what was happening to me, I began to have symptoms of a mental illness at a young age. When I was thirty years old, I got the diagnosis of Bipolar two Disorder. Living with a mental illness my whole life, I have had to hide it. I am still hiding it, and many of my friends do not know about my illness. The shame of letting other people know my "secret" was and is too much to bear.

I've worked in a mental health facility as a mental health professional for the past year. I have learned from working with people who had diagnoses of Schizophrenia, Bipolar one Disorder, Schizoaffective Disorder, and many other disorders that you can always come out of the other side of your trauma. It has been a transformative experience working with so many who have such a positive outlook on their lives and their illnesses. The illness did not define them; it was just a part of who they were. My time there made me realize I do not need to continue hiding behind my mask.

I came into the world a clean slate, and the rest was up to my parents to shape me into the person I grew up to be. I used to blame my father for my illness. I was so angry at the fact that the abuse made me the way that I am with a diagnosis of Bipolar. I now no longer set blame upon my father because through therapy I have chosen to not live in the anger I felt. I have empathy for the abusive experiences that he had encountered as a child, but I have also not forgotten what he did to me.

I want to get back to who I was before he took what was rightfully mine—my authentic self, which I am re-learning through the healing process of therapy and the right medication. I am still the kind, empathetic, funny, fun, good mother, wife, sister, daughter, also a good friend to those I have let get close to me.

Having a mental illness is not easy and it is something I struggle with every day. Unless you experience symptoms, it is hard to understand what the person who deals with them daily is going through. Family and friends unfamiliar with mental illness often struggle with how to cope with a loved one's symptoms and diagnosis. I remember a young woman in her twenties at the facility I worked at said to me, "For once I listened to my family about how they were affected by my mental illness; it wasn't until then, I realized how hard it had been for them. Then I saw it from their perspective. Then our relationships changed. I always made it about me. I just needed to listen."

The takeaway I want you to have after reading this book is that living life while managing symptoms of a mental illness is a process. We have choices of how we choose to cope with the things that happen to us in life. We can have dysfunctional, avoidant behaviors and blame the world for our own pain. Or we can choose to do the internal work to heal our hearts and minds. I am choosing to do the internal work. I am so tired of living with the ups and downs of guilt, shame, and self-doubt. As I have written this book, I have experienced a cathartic release of emotions that are helping set me free.

If you are reading this book, I hope you see a part of yourself in my writing. Many people experience symptoms of mental illness without even realizing it throughout their life. I would have been so grateful to have read something that I identified with as a young person or even as an adult. I am hopeful my book will bring awareness regarding mental illness, and I want whoever is reading this to feel accepted and validated in their thoughts and feelings.

My story is one of the underdog. I did not let the darkness take over the light that was always waiting for me.

I was told by a close friend that, "Pain transfers into art." This book is my art.

CHAPTER 1

THE NIGHT THAT CHANGED EVERYTHING

———

When I was fourteen years old, I was your typical teenager. I had a lot of friends, and I was always on the go, hanging out with my girlfriends at the movies, talking on the phone, having boyfriends, and most importantly making sure my parents were not interrupting my social life.

I was getting in trouble a lot at this age; I had a big mouth and I thought I knew it all. I started talking back to my parents. Little did I know this would make my teenage life a living hell. I would be grounded, which meant I could not watch TV, talk on the phone, or go out and be with my friends. This made me so angry because all I wanted to do was be social and have fun. I did not want to sit in my room bored all day and night. I especially did not want to hang out with my parents on a Friday or Saturday night. Let's be honest. That is every teenager's nightmare.

One night when I was grounded, my father came home to get tomato juice. I was alone in the house and my mother was across the street at the neighbors' house. My older and younger sister were also out of the house that evening.

My father said to me, "Who drank all of the tomato juice!" in a loud, annoyed, and stern voice that would scare a small child.

I looked up smug and pissed off. "Me, why?"

My father looked at me with hate in his eyes. "You asshole, why would you drink that? I needed it for Bloody Mary's with the neighbors."

"Fuck you, asshole," I replied. Those words set off the most traumatic night of my entire life.

My father came toward me. He was six-foot-one and about two hundred pounds at the time while I was five-foot-four and around one hundred pounds. In my head I heard the voice that your subconscious uses to tell you when you are in trouble scream at me, "*Run!*" So, I ran.

He chased me and pushed me down on the stairs. I screamed at the top of my lungs, "What are you going to do? Hit me? Go ahead! I fucking hate you!"

So, he did.

With a full fist, my father punched me out cold.

I saw black and then white stars, like lights in the cartoons when the cat was hit with a bat. After the stars came blackness, and then I came to. My father stood over me and I tried to crawl up the stairs away from him, tears streaming down my face. He grabbed my hair and pulled me up the flight of stairs with it. I remember thinking, *I hate him. I wish he were dead. Why is no one coming to save me?* When we got to the top of the stairs, I managed to run down them past him.

He was raging like a fire had been set inside of his soul. I ran out the front door with no coat and no shoes. It was the dead of winter in the suburbs of Chicago and thirty degrees with snow and ice on the stoop of the house. He locked me out and stood there staring at me.

As I was standing outside in a lightweight long sleeve shirt and leggings, I thought, *I cannot believe this is happening.* I just kept imagining different scenarios in my head of me trying to run. I contemplated running across the street to get my mother, but as though my body was paralyzed, and I could not move. I was in a state of trauma but did not understand at the time what was happening to me. I realized it was too cold and I was not wearing any shoes, so I could not bring myself to run. Plus, my eye was swollen shut and I did not know if I could compose myself in front of our neighbors.

I had just seen the movie *Misery* with Kathy Bates and I remember the main character flicking her off. As I stood outside freezing, I looked at him through the glass, flicked him off, and mouthed, "Fuck you." He just smirked as if me flicking him off did not matter at all.

Outside I was bold, fearless and hateful, just wanting this man who happened to be my father to release me from this hell. Inside I was just a terrified fourteen-year-old wanting her mother to come home and save her.

He opened the door and pulled me inside by the arm. My heart was pounding, and it felt as though it would come out of my chest. The reality that I could not escape terrified me. For the next hour he beat me, and verbally abused me. There was no way for me to reach my mother. I so desperately wanted to reach her so she could save me in this moment.

As my father was on top of me choking me until I was blue in the face, I managed to whisper, "You are killing me. Let me go, please." I really thought my own father was going to kill me in this moment. In a sort of out of body experience, I imagined what it would look like for my mother to walk into my house and find me lying there dead on the floor.

In that moment something snapped in my father's eyes, as if he suddenly realized, *Holy shit, I am going to kill her if I do not release this grip on her neck.* He got off me, pulled the phone out of the wall, threw it at me and said, "Go call your fucking mother."

I ran toward another phone with my eye swollen shut, and I called my mother. In this moment, I thanked whoever was watching over me above for not letting me die. I felt so afraid of what had happened that I was shaking. My mind was on hyper-speed trying to gather the thoughts of the madness that had taken over my father. I looked down at my striped shirt and my mind registered that the white stripe had blood splattered on it. I felt throbbing in the eye that my father had punched, and my nose was bleeding. It felt surreal. I felt physical pain, but what felt even greater was the emotional pain that followed.

I gathered myself in a quiet moment in my mind and then said hysterical but quietly, "Mom, Dad hurt me. Please come home."

She said, "I'm coming now." Then she hung up the phone.

I did not know where my father was in the house at the time, and I was so afraid he would come back to hurt me. I ran to my bathroom I shared with my sisters and put myself in between the toilet and the wall like a safety net to coddle me in my moment of utter terror.

My mother came home and asked my father where I was. I could not make out what he had said to her. When she found me, she said, "Are you okay? Oh my god, what happened?" I just sobbed in my mother's arms. My teenage brain could not process the trauma that had just occurred. I was in a state of shock.

My mother cleaned me up and helped me change clothes. As I stood outside my parents' room, my mother was screaming, "If you ever touch her again, I will divorce you!"

The next day my mom put a cover-up on my black eye and said to me, "It only happened once."

In that moment my teenage brain did not understand why my mom would say this to me. As if it was ok it had happened at all. Little did I know, when my mother was growing up, her father beat her and her siblings. This was why she had said this to me. I realize now as an adult of forty-four years that trauma marries trauma most times. It's the cycle of abuse, so they say. She then told me to take the day and hang out with friends. My father had convinced my sisters and mother that what had happened that night was not as bad as I claimed.

It was not until my parents divorced when I was twenty-three that my sisters and mom realized I was telling the truth. He never beat me to that level again, but he would slap me occasionally, covertly sexualize, and verbally abuse me until the age of forty. That is when I escaped the mental torment of the man, I call my father.

CHAPTER 2

CRAZY

When I was five years old, I had huge brown eyes, curly brown hair, and a wonderful sense of humor. I had a softness about me, a vulnerability. I was free-spirited and loved to explore. My biggest worry at this age was how long I was able to ride my bike outside. Or when I could play with my neighborhood friends. I do not have any memories before the age of five of any chaos in my life.

The chaos began once I started witnessing my parents fighting. It would start quietly with angry words exchanged from both my parents. Then it would explode as if they were throwing grenades at one another. My mother would scream as my father would scream over her. Then they would follow each other around the house yelling at one another and slamming doors.

My mother and father would be in a verbal battle for sometimes an hour or more; it was utter chaos. I would always watch and listen to the battle that ensued. Many times, I would try to get in between them to try and "save" my mom.

As you would expect that always turned out horribly. My father would scream in my face to get away.

My father was a ticking time bomb. He would come home from work at 6 p.m. Before he walked through the door, my mom and I had an ongoing inside joke wondering whether the "monster" would be home or the nice guy? It was a toss-up daily with us walking on eggshells not knowing who we were going to get that night.

If he were the "monster" he would be impatient, mean, abusive, irritable, demanding, and isolating. If he were the "nice guy" he would be engaging, fun, funny, easy going, and charming.

Imagine, living with a man who acted only two ways, no grey area. It was truly maddening, like a constant game of Russian Roulette that you did not want to play. This was always confusing for my childhood brain. I felt frightened and on edge when my father was around.

My young five-year-old self did not understand when my mom would leave the house when they were fighting. I could not wrap my head around her leaving me with "the monster." I would cry hysterically running outside on the driveway chasing her car, tears streaming, helplessly begging her not to leave me there. She would look at me so sadly and then just drive away.

I would wipe my tears with my little hands and go back into the house and into my room. My father would ignore me when I walked in from the garage. He would not engage or give me comfort in the moment I needed it most. I had to comfort my five-year-old self into a calm state alone. I would lie on my bed in a fetal position crying until my little body and mind felt calm again.

Over the years the fighting continued. It was not until the age of eight that the next phase of abuse occurred. This is when my father began to verbally abuse me. He would get angry with me for being annoying, talking too much, or just being in his way.

As a child I loved to talk, so I talked a lot. I was trying to talk myself into my parents' conversation one day when my father screamed at me, "Drew, be quiet! Drew, you are just talking to hear your own voice. Be quiet!"

I would then say, "Do you want to hear what my friend and I did?"

My father would yell at me the famous words that to this day are my trigger words: "Be quiet! *You're crazy!*"

I responded to this by continuing to talk enough to get a rise out of him, knowing that he would continue to rage at me.

My mom would say, "Don't say that to Drew. That is hurtful and not nice to say to our daughter."

"Oh please, she is just talking to talk. It is making me crazy!"

I don't think he realized how damaging the word "crazy" would become for me. I don't think he ever thought twice about his actions toward me. He himself as a child had been verbally abused. This was a learned behavior. He was mirroring what his parents had done to him.

My eight-year-old mind would try to process that word "crazy." Any time I had heard this word as a child it was on TV when someone was acting out of sorts. Like in a cartoon, when the mouse was spinning around and around all "crazy;" this was my childhood interpretation of this word. The definition of crazy is Not mentally sound: marked by the thought or action that lacks reason.[1]

It was a blessing in disguise as a child that I did not realize what this word meant. It was a blessing because I did not understand that he was hurting me emotionally. I just thought that he was using a mean word. My childhood brain did not process the full meaning of the word crazy until I grew older. When I grew older, I looked up the word to see what it meant, the actual definition, and then it made more sense to me. If I knew when I was young what this meant I would have felt so sad about myself, and my self-esteem would have suffered.

As I grew older, I learned this was an abusive word he used to describe me as a human being, a person. "Children exposed to family violence or abuse show the same pattern of activity in their brains as soldiers exposed to combat."[2]

Children's brains adapt to abuse and violence that is threatening to them. My brain when I was little was protecting me from my father's words. Protecting me from the verbal emotional combat my father was throwing at me. Children's brains, "They're primed to perceive threat and anticipate pain, adaptations that may be helpful in abusive environments but produce long-term problems with stress and anxiety."[3]

His verbal abuse became a frequent occurrence. I began to feel as though I was worthless when I was eight years old, and my self-esteem dwindled. I questioned if my father was right. After many times being called crazy throughout my youth, my brain was finally beginning to understand what this meant.

I then began to question the word that he was using and if it really pertained to me. Was I crazy? This was the beginning of me feeling anxiety that was never present before. Now the verbal abuse would affect how I was feeling about myself. I began to question my self-concept. "Early emotional abuse may permanently alter the brain's ability to use serotonin, a neurotransmitter that helps produce feelings of well-being and emotional stability."[4]

Every year on Thanksgiving my parents would invite the family over. During Thanksgiving when I was ten years old, I was walking room to room thinking. *No one likes me in this family; they all think I am annoying.* That was not the case. I was loved by my family cousins, aunts, grandparents; they all loved me and enjoyed having me around.

I knew my family and extended family loved me because they always showered me with love and affection through their words and actions toward me. I just could not shake my father's words to me. I convinced myself that I was not wanted or good enough.

I began to have obsessive thoughts and had a tough time sleeping at night. I never verbalized this to my mother or anyone for that matter. Why would I say anything? Anytime I had told my parents something I never felt I had any validation. I was always "exaggerating."

I internalized the reel in my mind of all the mean things that my father was spewing at me. I began to have traits of obsessive-compulsive disorder.

I would touch door handles and count how many times I would touch them. I would turn on and off light switches obsessively. I felt shame doing this. It felt unnatural and weird. At the same time, I felt if I did not do these things something bad would happen.

I started to smell my fingers obsessively and washing them. This gave me relief from the mental torment that I was experiencing. Doing this really bothered me, and the habit was short-lived. My sister and mom would imitate me doing it and laugh. I would laugh along with them, but inside I was ashamed and embarrassed about this behavior.

When I woke up for middle school, I also had a daily routine. Nothing was ever out of place. I would make sure my room was cleaned up and everything was put away perfectly. I would have a routine in the shower with the way I washed my body. I would count how many times the soap washed my arms, legs, etc. I felt relief, as if I had a say in something.

My emotional regulation was also definitely an issue. I was not talking about my feelings; I was just masking them. I grew up also having cognitive issues in school. In third grade, I was tested and assessed for a learning disability. I was struggling in school academically. I had a severe learning disability in math. I also would have issues with processing certain information. I never correlated the academic issues with the abuse that I had been experiencing until I was an adult. "Emotional abuse negatively affects a child's psychological and emotional development and may have long-term, negative effects on a child's cognitive development."[5]

Attachment was also an issue for me in middle school. Always daydreaming of wanting boyfriends. Having my first "boyfriend" in fifth grade. Always wondering when I would tire of that relationship and find myself a new one. Reading back through old diaries, I see now that I was always wanting male attention.

Diary entry October 10, 1986 (eleven years old)
Dear Diary, today was a good day. Mike talked to me.
WOW! I think Pat likes me. He is annoying! I think he
is going to ask me out tomorrow, but I do not know.

Diary entry March 7, 1986 (eleven years old)
Dear Diary, there is a boy in my school. He is so cute.
His name is Michael. I talked to him at the play Annie.
It was good. I want to kiss him now. I am going to dance
because I am excited.

Diary entry February 9, 1987 (twelve years old)
Dear Diary, I love Russ. He is so cute. DREW LOVES
RUSS!

Diary entry February 4, 1988 (thirteen years old)
Dear Diary, today is a good day. Russ is so mean now
I cannot believe I used to like him! I like Joe but he
hardly knows me.

There was a clear common thread of being obsessed with boys. This would go on my whole life until I got married. I was trying to fill the void of not having a male figure in my life. "Fathers provide their daughters with a masculine example. They help put their daughters at ease with other men throughout their lives. So, if a daughter does not grow up with the proper example, she will have less insight and be more likely to go for a man that will replicate the abandonment of her father."[6]

As the years passed, I turned into a tween. When I was twelve years old, I was skinny, lanky, with big, curly, shoulder-length, mahogany brown hair. My nose began to widen and looked too big for my small face. My eyes were deep brown almost black when you looked at them. I was outgoing and had a lot of friends in middle school. I was not as soft and vulnerable as I had been as a young child. I was now guarded and aware of the damage my father was inflicting on me. I was always in fight or flight mode when I was at home with him. I avoided being around him. I was either in my room listening to music, talking on the phone with friends, or watching TV in a room he would not be in or nearby.

When I was spending time together with my friends, I never told any of them what I was experiencing at home. I painted the pretty picture of my family to my friends, always making my family life better than it was for me when it came to my father's and my relationship. I was holding on to "the secret" of the abuse. Being with my friends made me feel safe and happy. At the time, I was grateful for having them. It was my escape.

I did not spend that much time alone with my father as a tween. One afternoon he asked me to go to the city with him. I did not want to go, but I went anyway. My father had convinced me that we would have a wonderful time.

We were walking on a city street when a beautiful woman walked by, and my dad was staring at her. I asked, "Daddy, why are you staring at that woman?"

"Drew, don't look at what I am looking at!"

My heart started pounding and my cheeks turned red and flushed. I felt ashamed and embarrassed for asking an honest question.

I was the "observer" and the "secret keeper." I was always watching what he was doing. I knew he was up to no good and he knew this. Being yelled at in public was humiliating for me and I was silent the rest of that day.

My father asked me on the ride home, "Why are you so quiet?"

I replied, "I am just tired."

I stared out the window as he was driving home, replaying in my mind what had happened on the street. I felt uneasy and upset the whole ride home. When we came back home, I did not tell my mother what had happened.

The abuse accelerated. When I was twelve my father began slapping me in my face occasionally. He never did this when my mother was around. I honestly cannot tell you the details of when and where. I have blocked out in my mind the exact moments when he did this to me. I just have "flashes" of these moments, basically me having a movie reel in my mind of my dad slapping my face. There are no specific details to the flash of the memory that I see.

I felt that if I had a big mouth, it would make him think I was not afraid of him. I never told my mom that he would hit me in my face. I feared her thinking I was exaggerating. He always convinced her I was lying. This was just another secret kept that I had to hold inside along with all the other abuse secrets that were piling up.

CHAPTER 3

TRANSFORMATION

———

My mother, father, and I sat in the waiting room of a plastic surgeon's office when I was fifteen years old. I remember thinking, *I am going to have a small nose and look so much better!* Little did I know my mother already knew I would not only need a nose job, but a chin job as well. She did not speak of the chin because she did not want me to feel badly; she would rather have the doctor break the news.

I felt lucky that I had parents who would help me change the one thing about my appearance that bothered me. My nose was too big for my small face and in middle school I was bullied for it.

One boy in my group of friends would say to me, "You have a Jew nose. It is huge!"

My comeback to this boy would be, "Just you wait, in high school I will get it fixed. How are you going to change your ugly face?"

I was taught this technique of "verbal assault" from my father. It came in handy when necessary, and I was not afraid to use it to stick up for myself.

We were called back to a room. I got on the table and the doctor said, "Well, she has a good profile. We just need to thin out the nose because it is wide. Drew also needs a chin implant to give her a nice profile." I thought, *What the hell do I need a chin for?*

I asked my mom why she hadn't told me about my chin. She laughed and said, "You will look beautiful."

So that winter break I had a rhinoplasty and a chin implant. After the procedures, I felt a sort of transformation within myself. The subtle changes on my face made me feel more confident. I felt surer of myself and less self-conscious about my appearance as a teenager. When I would put my make up on in the morning, I would look in the mirror and I really liked what I saw looking back at me. This refection of myself felt attractive and fitting to what I was always wanting when I looked in the mirror.

I had always been an attractive girl, but this would make me a "better version of myself." Let's just say, it elevated my dating game.

When I went back to school after winter break, the boys and girls noticed something had changed. They said, "You look so pretty. What is different?" I explained to them that over break I had a nose job. There was never any judgment from the kids at school about my face, only positive feedback. As we all know, high school kids can be brutal. I was grateful that I was not bullied for changing my appearance. At least to my face, there was no judgment. Behind my back I am not sure what the kids at school said about me. Every high school girl I knew would look at magazines, discussing what parts of their face and body that they wanted to change about themselves.

After my surgery, my own father began to covertly sexualize me. My father would comment on how beautiful I looked and would stare at me. Not the stare a loving father gives a daughter. The kind of stare that made me feel uncomfortable.

My father never touched me sexually. Reading all the research I now know for certain I was covertly sexualized. Covert sexual abuse is more subtle. "Covert sexual abuse is surreptitious, indirect, sexualized use or abuse of a child by a parent, stepparent, or any other long-term caregiver." "It's commonly referred to as emotional incest or covert incest because it involves indirect (not hands-on) sexuality that is implied or suggested rather than physically acted out."[7]

I had many experiences with my father of covert sexual abuse. These are the memories of some of them that I remember.

I was a huge fan of Cindy Crawford workout tapes in the nineties. When I was sophomore in high school, I would do the workout tapes in our basement. We had a huge TV, and my father would sit on the couch and watch me while commenting on Cindy Crawford's body and looks. At the time I did not realize fully that my father was also watching my body, making comments about how my body was just as good Cindy Crawford's. I had in this moment a disgusted feeling inside. He never spoke like this to me in front of my mother and sisters. Only when we were alone would he talk to me in this manner.

I felt in this moment that although there was no sexual touch from my father, my father was invading my personal boundaries by discussing my body.

My family was upstairs during this encounter. This was the story of my life. No one around to witness what was happening to me. I never told anyone about this as I felt too embarrassed and ashamed. After I finished the tape, I walked upstairs to the shower. I stood under the water in disgust, feeling as though I was washing off the sin of what transpired in the basement.

Growing up in high school I was looked at as the well-off girl, socially in it, who had her shit together, a charmed life. I would drive to school in my new car that my parents bought me when I got my license. I had perfectly coiffed hair, perfectly done makeup, nice clothing. On the outside I was "put together" when on the inside I was screaming.

I always hoped that one day I could free myself from the "monster." I just wanted to get away from him. I felt constantly stressed and anxious, waiting for the next time my father would rage at me or say something to make me feel uncomfortable. Little did anyone at my high school know that I was living in a cycle of abuse.

During the summer months of sophomore year going into junior year, I invited my girlfriends to come over to lie in the sun. I would watch as my father was watching us lying there in our bikinis. When my father was watching us, I would think, *please God, don't let my friends see my dad.* I was so disgusted, and I had no control over what he was doing. They never noticed. They were too busy listening to music and gossiping. I was so grateful.

When I was in my thirties and I was at a family event, I was talking to our old neighbor who had lived across the street from my mother and father when we were growing up. He told me that when my father was watching us in the summer when I had my friends over, my father had said to him, "Don't they look hot in those bikinis?"

The neighbor replied to my father by saying, "You do realize you are talking about your own daughter?"

My father of course had no response. The neighbor was repulsed by his behavior. I felt validation in this moment as he told me this. Finally, someone witnessed what I had experienced so many times in my life with him.

Every Christmas growing up, our family would take lavish vacations. My mother, father, two sisters and I went on a cruise one year. When the ship stopped at the port, my mom and sisters were walking around browsing in a store. I was standing with my father, and he said, "Do you want to know how I lost my virginity?"

I remember thinking, *why is my own dad talking about losing his virginity?*

I felt extremely uncomfortable with this conversation, but I said, "If you want to tell me, I guess." My father in explicit detail continued to talk about losing his virginity with a prostitute at the age of sixteen.

I felt embarrassed and ashamed. I stood there and listened as he smirked. As he was recounting the experience, I could see in his face as he shared, like he was reliving it. After hearing him tell me this, I felt dirty listening to my own father talk about his first sexual encounter.

"The lack of boundaries of covert incest even though there is no sexual touch the relationship feels 'icky' to the child—too close for comfort. The lack of boundaries creates an incestuous feeling, and the child feels trapped."[8]

That is what my father was doing to me on this vacation. I felt exactly that, trapped with no escape from the sexual details I was forced to listen to.

I did not tell my mother about this encounter with my father. Every child has "their own reality." The sad part about this is the reality was I was being covertly sexualized by my own father. That was the truth period, not my "childhood reality."

Another Christmas vacation we went to Puerto Rico. I was in my early twenties. One day we had gone to the beach as a family, and my sisters and mother were in the water. Just my father and I were on the beach. My father looked at me and said, "Your boyfriend is so lucky. You have the best body." No matter how many times he did or said something inappropriate, I still was in shock at his behavior toward me. I do not remember what I said to him after he told me that. I do know I walked away feeling a pit in my stomach. I knew once again he had covertly sexualized me, when there was not a person in ear shot.

Through the years, he was getting away with this behavior, with no consequence for his actions. Never once did I speak of this until I was older in therapy. Then I realized the covert sexual abuse that was happening to me made me hypersexual growing up.

The hypersexuality began in middle school. I was in sixth grade and had a boyfriend named Brett. This was my first French kiss. I specifically remember feeling a warmth in my body, a reaction to the intimate sexual connection with a boy. I loved how this made me feel inside. I did not realize that what I really was craving was "normal" attention from my own father. I wanted my father to have conversations about my everyday life, school, friends, and hobbies instead of surface conversations. I wanted connection with my father, just attention in general that was "normal." That was what I was craving.

In eighth grade, I slept at my friend's house with about four girlfriends. Our guy friends snuck over to her house. One of the boys at the time was my boyfriend. I went outside with him and as we were kissing, he went up under my shirt. The same feeling, I had with my first real kiss happened when this boy touched my body. It was a surge of warmth and then a feeling of wanting more. This was a huge deal at the time; being in middle school, "hooking up" with your boyfriend and how far you went was always the topic of conversation. Going to second base was major in eighth grade.

When my mom picked me up from the sleepover that morning, I got into the car, and she had asked how my night was. I told her how Jared had gone up my shirt. She was not pleased and grounded me for doing this. My mom said, "When you go away to overnight camp, if I find out a guy is going up your shirt you are in big trouble."

My mother's reaction to hearing about my sexual encounters with boys did not affect my ability to tell her about the covert sexualization that I was experiencing with my father. I thought of these as two separate things at the time.

I did not tell her about my father and the sexualization because of two things:

1. I felt she wouldn't believe me because my dad always made it out like I was lying to her.
2. I felt ashamed and guilty about the covert sexualization.

I could not wrap my head around what my father was saying to me. So, I kept it a secret from her. I felt that it was somehow my fault that he kept talking to me this way, that I never said to him that I did not like when he spoke that way to me. I began to believe that I was making a "big deal" out of nothing.

I would not let another boy touch my body until the first year in high school. This is when my hypersexuality exploded. I hooked up with a lot of guys I thought were cute. Sophomore year I was dating a guy I fell hard for. He was one year older than me and I was hooked.

I had been grounded one night when I was supposed to go to a party with him. My best friend at the time, Yvette, told me that she would call me to give me details of the evening. Yvette called me from the party, and she sounded so upset. I asked her what was going on. She said, "Rob is having sex with Jessica in a bedroom."

My heart sank and I felt physically sick inside. Due to the fact I was sexually intimate with this boy, I could not fully wrap my brain around the pain from hearing this news. I felt that because I was sexually intimate with him that he cared for me enough to not cheat on me with another girl.

I equated being intimate to love with this boy. I was sadly mistaken. Obviously, we broke up; he broke up with me for her. My teenage brain was not emotionally developed enough to deal with these feelings or the sexual experiences I was having with him. I was too young to understand the difference between lust and love.

I also was not equating the need for my own father's attention. I desperately wanted a normal father-daughter relationship in my life. My friend's fathers were emotionally present in their lives, and it made a difference in how they did not constantly need male validation and attention.

I would continue to go on and date constantly. One boy after the next I would "hook up with." I also would hook up with my guy friends, and other guys I thought were attractive. I would not get emotionally involved with these boys. It was purely sexual to me, which was all I wanted. I did not want to chance the feeling of the heartbreak I had with Rob.

I also kept everything I was doing on the "down low." I knew if anyone at school really knew what I was doing with these guys, I would get the reputation of being a slut. I had two more serious relationships in high school. One of the boys ended up cheating on me.

The other boyfriend did not cheat. He was my first "love", and we were best friends before we were dating. I spent a lot of time with him, and he treated me well. He cared for me on many levels, and I deeply cared for him. When I later went to college, I was overwhelmed by other guys' attention toward me, and I ended up breaking up with him.

My whole high school experience was filled with many sexual encounters. I was hooked to the feeling of being wanted. I believe the covert sexualization from my father affected my sexuality as an adolescent since the "victims of covert sexualization think they are nothing more than a sexual object for other people to use for whatever they want."[9]

I was rarely emotionally vulnerable with boys. I kept it on a sexual plane to not get too emotionally attached to the boys I was "hooking up" with. I felt as if I had a power over the boys, I was with because I was good at being sexual and giving and receiving sexual pleasure. It was an unhealthy way of receiving and giving attention.

I never spoke to anyone about these sexualized incidents in detail until I was in therapy in my early twenties. I was going to a male therapist. After telling him about the experiences I had growing up and was still having with my father, he told me that I had been covertly sexualized by my father. I did not believe him when he told me this. I thought because I was not being physically touched, it did not make any sense.

This male therapist also sexualized me. I would go to his home for our sessions. We would meet on his porch some days. I came to our scheduled appointment one day, wearing a tight t-shirt. He looked at me and said, "Did your boobs get bigger?"

"What did you just say to me?"

"I am asking you if your boobs got bigger because they look like they did."

I was in shock. "I don't know." I sat through the session feeling disgusted about how this male therapist talked to me. It was an all too familiar feeling, like the feeling I had when my father spoke to me that way.

I called that male therapist that night. I told him what he had said to me was wrong and inappropriate. He did not even apologize. It was an awkward conversation, but I was proud of myself for being brave enough to stand up for what was rightfully mine, for myself respect, which I gained back in that moment. I called him out on his disgusting behavior toward me. I did not go back to see him again.

It was not until I was in my thirties that I began seeing a female therapist. She explained to me in one of our sessions that I was indeed covertly sexualized. I believed her because I had done research on this subject. I then understood what my father had been doing all those years. I finally felt validation from this therapist, and I felt some settling inside of me, that now I could finally deal with how I had behaved sexually all those years. There was a reason I was the way I was with boys and men growing up. She made me realize that what had been happening with my father was not my fault. I will be forever grateful to that therapist, for I finally had a voice.

CHAPTER 4

FLASH

I was showered and ready to go to my afternoon classes, and I walked through campus waving to my friends and acquaintances. Around the quad in the spring and summer, students would be sitting under the trees socializing. On this day during my freshman year at university, I was in a good mood with the thoughts of what homework that I had to do for my classes.

As I was walking and thinking of the plans my friends and I had made for that weekend. I looked forward to the weekends; they were so much fun. It was a time for my friends and me to not focus on our schoolwork and just have fun.

The private university I went to was small with about seven thousand students. Everyone knew everyone and when you walked to class there was not a day you would not see people you knew.

I got to the building for my education class, sat down at my desk, and took out my book, pen, notebook, waiting for the teacher to start the class. All the students took their seats and I said hello to the classmates I knew. The teacher began the lecture and midway through I had a flash of the night my father brutalized me.

I felt as if I was watching a movie reel right in front of my eyes, replaying moments of the events that occurred that night. The flash was of fourteen-year-old me sitting on the stairs, in the house I grew up in, the moment my father punched me out cold. I then saw myself running, trying to get away from him. A flash of the image of my father on top of me choking me. I was experiencing disassociation, which is when one detaches from reality.

The definition of disassociation is the act or process of dissociating: the state of being dissociated: such as: The separation of whole segments of the personality (as in multiple personality disorder) or of discrete mental processes (as in the schizophrenias) from the mainstream of consciousness or of behavior.[10] My body felt numb and heavy as if it was weighted down by sand. Emotionally I felt so overwhelmed, overcome with sadness and fear. For many people, dissociation is a natural response to trauma that they cannot control. It could be a response to a one-off traumatic event or ongoing trauma and abuse.

CAUSES OF DISSOCIATION.

TRAUMA.

You may psychologically disconnect from the present moment if something bad happens to you. This is called peritraumatic dissociation. Experts believe this is a technique your mind uses to protect you from the full impact of the upsetting experience you had.[11]

I was having an out of body experience and I was watching myself outside of myself. Those three specific events were playing out in my mind and felt so real to me, as if they were happening right then. I said to myself, "Why is this happening now? How can I make this stop?" I was wondering if anyone in my class noticed what I was experiencing. If you were to look at me, I looked as if I was spacing out. I was looking straight ahead and was completely not present within myself.

As quickly as the flashes came, they were gone. They went away and I "came to" so to speak. I got up from my seat with tears in my eyes. I walked out of class and went straight to my dorm room. My roommate was not there when I got back as she was at class. I dropped all my books on my desk, sat on our couch, lit a cigarette, and cried. I thought I had put the memories from four years prior away in a secret compartment inside of my brain. I had to figure out a way to cope with the post-traumatic stress I was experiencing. That day I chose not to discuss with anyone what had occurred in class—not my roommate, family, or anyone.

I continued with my daily routines as if the flash had never happened. Many people with post-traumatic stress disorder struggle to cope with flashbacks and disassociation, which may occur because of encountering triggers, that is, reminders of a traumatic event. "A flashback may be temporary, and you may maintain some connection with the present moment, or you may lose all awareness of what's going on around you, being completely back into your traumatic event."[12]

This was exactly what occurred to me that day. I lost all sense of awareness of what had been going on in the class. I was back in that traumatic event. That was the only time I had experienced a flashback when I was at university.

I lived with an amazing girl named Miriam. She was one of the first people I met at school. The first night at university I was outside of the dorms smoking a cigarette. Miriam was also outside sitting on a stoop. I walked up to her and said, "Hey, my name is Drew. What's yours?"

She replied, "Hey, I'm Miriam. Sit with me, and we can smoke together."

From that moment on we were fast friends. I sat down and we talked about where we were from. Our likes, dislikes, what classes we were taking. It was an instant connection of friendship. Talking to Miriam was easy and fun. She became one of my closest friends. We would also end up joining the same sorority at school.

Miriam was from Kentucky; she spoke with an accent I called a "country twang." That always made her laugh. She would in return, make fun of my Chicago accent; it was our own inside joke. Miriam was one of the kindest people I had met. She was always so much fun to be around. She never judged anyone for anything. She was just a free spirit, who was liked by anyone who met her. Her charming warm personality made it impossible not to like her.

We decided the first year to be roommates second semester. It was a roommate match made in heaven. We would stay up late many nights, smoking, listening to music, and talking. We respected one another's boundaries and never had any issues. We enjoyed one another's company, and it was just easy to co-habituate.

One evening we were painting our loft in our dorm room. I remember out of nowhere I started crying. I felt that inside my body and brain something was off. I felt a blackness inside of me I had felt before. I felt this when I lived at home after the beating from my father. Miriam said, "Are you okay? What is wrong? Talk to me."

I said, "Oh my god. I am so tired. We are up late all of the time."

Miriam and I were so open and honest with one another so there would be no reason for her to question me. We were always out drinking at the bars until one or two in the morning, or we would be spending time together in the dorms with friends smoking and talking up until four in the morning some nights, so she bought it.

I was so relieved that Miriam did not actually see I was having my first depressive episode. I had a way of acting as if I was okay by making up excuses to why I was tired. Miriam was also terribly busy with her schoolwork and classes, so she was not focused on how I was behaving. I always had a way of masking how bad I was feeling so she would not be concerned. During a depressive episode, one often has "the inability to experience pleasure, fatigue or loss of energy, sleep problems, weight loss, concentration or memory problems, feelings of worthlessness or guilt."[13]

The stress of me being away at school had triggered post-trau-matic stress and my Bipolar two Disorder. Stressful events, such as going away to college or moving, are known to trigger bipolar disorder, particularly in people already genetically vulnerable to developing it.[14]

I worked through that depressive episode for a week. I did this by self-medicating, binge drinking to numb the emo-tions of my sadness, chain smoking to relieve the anxiety I had been feeling—without realizing smoking was making my anxiety worse. I was hooking up with random guys who had an interest in me. I noticed by doing all these dysfunctional behaviors the depressive episode would lift. By distracting myself from the depressive feelings my brain was forced to focus on things other than depression, such as the pleasure of being intoxicated, sexual gratification, and being social daily.

Looking back, I do not know how I am still alive. One night the first year we went to a fraternity party at a fraternity house on campus. My sorority went to this event every year. The theme of the party ironically was The Funeral Exchange. Everyone in my sorority wore black as if we were going to a funeral. All the guys from the fraternity wore black as well. I wore a tight black long sleeve shirt with wide leg black pants with suspenders and black chunky shoes that were very nineties style. I had my hair perfectly diffused with a lot of eye makeup, and deep brown lipstick. I was ready to party that evening.

I walked in with Miriam and four other friends. The guys said to us, "Girls, let's do around the world. In each room there are shots. Let's go!" So, we all went from one room to the next. I took shot after shot, not thinking of the consequences that would come later. I had not eaten a lot before the party because I wanted to get drunk. I consumed fourteen shots in one hour. At first it felt like I was having the best time. I was laughing with the guys and my friends. Then all the sudden I was very intoxicated, and the room began to spin. I told my friends that I was going to the bathroom. I was so drunk that the hallway I was in was swaying back and forth.

I finally made it to the bathroom and began to vomit violently. I was around 102 pounds at the time, and my small figure could not hold this much hard liquor. I was vomiting for what seemed like an hour. When one of my friends found me in the bathroom, I was lying on the floor with my arm around the seat of the toilet. My head was halfway in the toilet itself. They realized how wasted I was, and knew they had to get me back to the sorority house.

I remember one of the fraternity boys picking me up and carrying me to the sorority house. I was put into one of the girls' bunkbeds. I was lying passed out when I woke up suddenly. The sheets and pillow I was lying on were soaking wet from me sweating. I felt very ill, and my body started convulsing. It was all such a blur because I was so intoxicated. I just remember the older sorority girls saying, "I think she needs to go to the hospital; it could be alcohol poisoning." Then I passed out.

I woke up to a nurse putting smelling salts to my nose in the ER of a hospital. I realized how lucky I was I did not die. The rest of that evening is a blur. I remember waking up the next morning in my bunk bed of my dorm room with no memory of how I got there. I was still drunk from the night before and I had a pounding headache. I had to call my mother to tell her what had happened. Apparently, I had been brought to the hospital in an ambulance and I had to tell my mom and dad because a bill was going to be coming to their house.

My mom picked up the phone. "Drew, is everything okay?"

"Mom, you are going to be very mad at me."

"Drew, what did you do?"

"I was at a fraternity party, and I was very drunk. I had to be taken to the hospital because they thought I had alcohol poisoning. An ambulance was called, and a bill will be coming to the house."

My mom was shocked and upset. Her voice sounded concerned. "Drew, you are lucky to be alive. I cannot believe how scary and irresponsible that behavior is."

I also had to tell my mother that I was also on academic probation. I had been partying and not going to most of my classes. My mom said, "Drew, either you get your grades up and stop drinking and going out all the time, or you have to come home."

In the back of my mind, I thought, *there is no way in hell I am going to go back home to be around my father.*

Let us just say, I got my shit together. The thought of being home with my father made me put everything in order quickly. I did not want to go back home to the abuse of my father. Being away from there was a sense of freedom. Not having to see him made me feel less anxiety and fear.

I began to go to class regularly instead of partying during the weekdays. I went to the school library and studied. My grades began to go up and I was finally taking school seriously. The arduous work was paying off and I got off academic probation second semester the first year. I would go out some Thursday nights but, mostly, I would go out on the weekend nights so I could study during the week.

HYPOMANIA

My first hypomanic episode, which entails "feeling unusually high or optimistic or extremely irritable, unrealistic, grandiose beliefs about one's abilities or powers, sleeping little, but feeling extremely energetic, talking so rapidly others can't keep up, racing thoughts."[15]

I experienced my first hypomanic episode after my friends, and I were watching our favorite show *Friends*. The episode that I experienced began when I wanted to cut off my hair to look like Monica. In the show Monica had super short hair and the girls in my sorority began to cut their hair to look like hers. I loved how Monica's hair looked and I decided that over winter break I would go home and cut off all my hair. I was obsessing about cutting my hair in this episode of hypomania. I had long dark curly hair that fell below my shoulders. It was beautiful. When I first came to school all the guys would always say to me, "I love your hair. It is so pretty."

My older sister, Devon, attended the same university with me. All the guys were "obsessed" with her. They would always say to me, "Your sister, Devon, is so hot!" She also had beautiful curly hair. When I came to school the first year everyone knew I was Devon's sister. I got extra attention because of this. The guys would say, "Drew you have a hot older sister, and you are hot too."

All the male attention triggered me. It was the same feeling as when my dad sexualized me. I felt the guys did not want to know me as a person, that I was just an object to them. A guy the first year sent me flowers with a note to my dorm room just to get my extra attention. I was flattered by the gesture, but it also made me feel uncomfortable as I also felt it was unwanted attention. I was asked out a lot and most of the time I would say no. I played it off as if I liked the attention, when I despised it. Internally, I wanted all the attention to go away, just like I wanted my father's attention to go away.

By me cutting off all my hair during winter break, I knew I would become invisible. I came back from the break and my friends were shocked. Not a good shocked either. My friend Miriam said, "Oh my god! You cut off all of your gorgeous hair!"

"I know. What do you think?"

"I mean, it sure is different."

I knew it was a huge topic of discussion. I looked not as pretty as I had. I could tell in my friends' faces that it was not a good change.

When I went to class that day, I ran into a guy friend of mine. "Holy shit, Drew! What did you do? You cut all your hot off. You were going to be in the fraternity calendar like your hot sister but not anymore."

I felt so embarrassed, and I could feel rage inside from how this guy had spoken to me. "Well, go fuck yourself. Did I ask your opinion about my hair? No, I did not. See you later."

I played it off as though I did not care when, I really did care. At the same time, I felt relief. All the attention now would be off me, and it was. The guys on campus no longer were calling my dorm room or asking me out like they had been before I cut my hair off. They would walk by me on campus and would just wave and keep walking. It was quite a shift from how it had been before.

RAGE
I had another side of hypomania in college that was toxic. Rage was built up inside of me from never having an outlet to discuss the abuse. My junior and senior year at school I would have such rage.

If an undergraduate in my sorority said something to me that was anything less than positive, I would lash out. I would lash out with such a vengeance that I would make her cry. I felt no remorse, just anger. I really was trying to treat someone how my father had treated me. It felt good to make others feel small and helpless to my rage.

A 2012 study and a 2014 study found that people with bipolar disorder show greater episodes of aggression than people without bipolar disorder. People who are not receiving treatment or those experiencing a rapid change in mood, or rapidly cycling between moods, are more likely to experience periods of irritability too.[16]

My senior year, I lived in an off-campus house with seven other girls. If I got into a fight with one of my friends, I would go into full-blown verbal rage. One specific time I fought with my friend Carly. It became so verbally explosive that all my friends I lived with thought it would be a clever idea if I went home for the weekend. They were all mad at me for how I had spoken to my friend Carly.

I left for the weekend feeling so embarrassed and ashamed about my behavior. I packed a weekend bag for home. I did not say goodbye to any of my friends. Thinking back to how I had treated my friend Carly, I cried on the two-and-a-half-hour ride home. I did not know any other way to have healthy coping skills. When I fought with my friends, I was mirroring the behaviors I was taught by my father growing up. When I walked in my parents' house, I told my mom I came home because I wanted a break from school. I never told her what had happened and how I treated my friend.

Due to the fact I never told any of my college friends what I had experienced growing up, they never understood where all my rage came from. Just this year, when I am now forty-four years old, I explained to my friend Miriam why I had behaved the way I had in college. She cried when I told her.

"Drew, I am so sorry you felt so sad and did not feel I could be there for you when we were young."

I said to her, "Miriam, you were always such a good friend. You still are. Thank you for being there for me now."

We cried together on that phone call. I am so grateful we are still friends to this day.

CHAPTER 5

DISASTROUS INDEPENDENCE

———

I was finally free to live on my own. I was twenty-two years old and starting the life of an independent working woman in Lincoln Park in Chicago, Illinois. My apartment was in a five-story walk-up building on a beautiful tree-lined street. It was four hundred square feet and eight hundred dollars a month. I could watch TV, cook (which I cannot do), and wash my hair all at the same time. I could not buy a bed because the space was so small. My parents had bought me a pullout couch to sleep and sit on. The size of my place did not matter because it was all mine and there was not a parent in sight. I had graduated from university with a BS in Psychology and was extremely excited to start my new career in social work.

While I was happy to be on my own, this was the beginning of some of the most fucked up years of my life.

I had just started a job at a mental health facility in Evanston, Illinois, as a Psychiatric Residential Service Coordinator. I worked with people with Schizophrenia, Bipolar one

Disorder, Schizoaffective Disorder, and more. You name the mental illness from the Diagnostic and Statistical Manual of Mental Disorders 5th Edition, and I worked with it. I loved this job and it made me feel like I had purpose. I had a caseload of forty-plus people ranging in age from twenty to seventy-five. I had daily individual meetings with the residents who lived in this facility. I remember an older gentleman sat across from me and said, "You are my caseworker? You are young enough to be my daughter."

I laughed and said, "Well, this is what you got. It is so nice to be working with you."

I always had a lightness in the way I spoke to the people I worked with. I knew they had to live at this residential mental health facility. I could leave at night and go home, but they could not.

Working in this environment made me feel "normal." I saw and worked with people with severe mental illness and my own symptoms paled in comparison, leading me to feel "normal." I had not been diagnosed yet, so I did not know I had Bipolar two Disorder. I did know deep inside that I had a mental illness; I just did not have a name for it yet. I realized this when I was working with a young man who had Bipolar one. His symptoms of mania and depression looked familiar to me but mine were not as severe.

"bipolar disorder, formally called manic depression, is a mental health condition that causes extreme mood swings that include emotional highs (mania or hypomania) and lows (depression)."

There are several types of bipolar and related disorders. They may include mania or hypomania and depression. Symptoms can cause unpredictable changes in mood and behavior, resulting in significant distress and difficulty in life. The difference between Bipolar one and Bipolar two is as follows:

Bipolar one disorder: *You have had at least one manic episode that may be preceded or followed by hypomanic or major depressive episodes. In some cases, mania may trigger a break from reality (psychosis).[17]*

Bipolar 2 disorder: *You have had at least one major depressive episode and at least one hypomanic episode, but you have never had a manic episode. I had experienced depressive episodes in college and after college.[18]*

"Mania and hypomania are two distinct types of episodes, but they have the same symptoms. Mania is more severe than hypomania and causes more noticeable problems at work, school, and social activities, as well as relationship difficulties. Mania may also trigger a break from reality (psychosis) and require hospitalization.

Both a manic and hypomanic episode include three or more of these symptoms: abnormally upbeat, jumpy, or wired. Increased activity, energy or agitation, exaggerated sense of well-being and self-confidence (euphoria), decreased need for sleep, unusual talkativeness, racing thoughts, distractibility, poor decision-making- for example, going on buying sprees, taking sexual risks, or making foolish investments."[19]

My hypomania was always tipping on the edge of mania but never went into full blown mania. Hypomania on me looks like I am hyper; I talk a lot and am over animated with my expressions. No one ever thought I was hypomanic when I was experiencing these symptoms. To others on the outside, I was always described as fun, outgoing, easy to have a good relationship with, spontaneous.

I had hypomania that would last days, and most times it was like an ebb and a flow. The ups and downs of my moods were all situational. At work my hypomania was slight and my moods were either elevated or more balanced. I would appear more balanced because I was focused on the tasks of my job such as paperwork, meetings with residents, and computer work as well.

A slightly higher elevated mood would occur when I was with men on dates, or if I was out with friends drinking at the clubs. When I drink is usually when hypomania is at a highest. Something with alcohol and symptoms is usually not a good mix for me and I become very chatty and grandiose. These moods would shift from a great mood into "too good of a mood."

When I was working at this job, I was making nineteen thousand dollars a year. I was never taught the value of a dollar. Let me rephrase. My parents taught me, but I did not give a shit to pay attention. So, when I was living on my own, I did not know how to pay a bill or manage a check book.

I would go shopping, writing checks and not realizing there was no money in my bank account. The store I bought clothes at would put my checks under the glass near the register that way whoever was working knew I was a "check bouncer." I would get my paycheck every two weeks. I would pay my rent in cash and then I would give my best effort to try to pay the bills I had. The rest of my money was blown on cigarettes and going to clubs with my friends.

I had another job on Saturday nights waitressing at an outside bar in the Gold Coast of Chicago. This combination was, let's just say, deadly for my mental health. I was rail thin and had the *Sliding Doors* haircut that Gwyneth Paltrow rocked in that movie. I had a great "look." I dressed in clothing that was alternative but minimal—tight black tank tops with low waisted jeans, always minimal sexy.

The attention from men when I worked at this bar was just like the attention the first year at university. This was a rush for me at the time. I did not feel like I had as a young girl getting this attention. I loved it, and I took advantage of the attention I received. I made eight hundred dollars in tips in eight hours when I worked. I would spend all the money the next day, mostly on clothing.

This was the beginning of new behaviors that did not manifest until I lived alone. The beginning of severe anorexia set in. I would go to Dunkin Donuts before work and get a black medium coffee and a blueberry muffin. Then at lunch time I would eat a salad. I would not eat anything else all day and night. No snacks, no dinner. Nothing day in and day out. I would starve. I was at the lowest weight that I had ever been as a young adult. The fact I smoked two packs of Marlboro Lights per day did not help either.

In my fridge there literally was not a morsel of food. I would buy cigarettes, pay my bills, and rent, and go clubbing. I never had money left for food. For me that was not high on the priority list. I also used men like you would use a phone book before technology existed. I would go out meet a guy and hook up, most of the time I would have sex with them, and after he would leave, I would call another guy to come over and have sex.

Looking back, I realized these behaviors were symptoms of hypomania and I was in the thick of getting a high from the sex that I was having with these men. At the time I thought, *Man, I just really am having a lot of sex.*

A guy once said to me, "All you want to do is fuck and eat pizza."

My response was, "What guy does not like fucking, and who does not like pizza?" I thought, *well okay that is not a normal guy.*

My behavior was not normal. When I was working at the mental health facility, I had a very attractive boss who was probably five years older than me. He would flirt with me. One day he came into my office, closed the door, and kissed me. No one at work knew that he and I were hooking up. We literally kissed and did nothing more.

I never slept with him because I was not that attracted to him. I had a type, which was usually tall, dark hair, light eyes, either green or blue, or dark eyes (that was mysterious to me), a nice build, confidence was key, and aggressive in the way that the guy knew how to take charge when it came to being sexual. My boss was not the typical type that I usually went for.

What I began to realize was that he was engaged to be married and he was cheating on his fiancée with me. He ended up telling me this when he brought me to a bar one day. At the time I did not care. I would make out with him, and he was hooked on me. He made me mix tapes and was completely smitten.

For him, I was the danger zone, the exciting woman in his life that his fiancée did not know about. He ended up leaving his fiancée for me. I told him I did not want a relationship. I had no care about his feelings. I was getting my needs met, so to speak. Plus, going to work was more fun because it was our secret.

When I told him, I did not intend to have a relationship with him, he was not happy at all. I began to feel he was critical about my work when I was doing a diligent job. His criticism was annoying, but in the end, I left that job to start a new career and work in foster care.

DEPARTMENT OF CHILDREN AND FAMILY SERVICES

My symptoms were not as severe as they were at my other job. I was constantly on the go at this job, and I did not have a lot of down time to sit and think, which in turn was good for my symptoms. I found myself less hypomanic and not as depressed due to being busy all the time. I also was eating during the day and not starving myself as I had been at my other job. On the weekends the hypomania was the same as it always had been. I still was meeting men to hook up with and I still was shopping like I had been.

I felt that I had to prove myself in this environment. All the women and men who worked there were very tight with one another. I was like the outsider in this office space I was just starting in. I felt comfort with the people I worked with and had respect for them because there was a sense of family.

Everyone in this work environment was quick to offer help when needed on certain cases and any other paperwork I needed help with. My colleagues really cared about how each of us were doing emotionally and how our personal lives were. Everyone was sincerely interested in how the people in the office were every day.

Working in foster care was a very cathartic job for me. By working with abused and neglected children, it helped me come to terms with the abuse I had gone through. I had so much empathy for the children I worked with. I knew that what I had gone through was not severe abuse, but I also realized that no matter how severe a child is abused, it takes a part of them away. The abuse takes the vulnerability of a child and puts that child in protective mode most of their lives. That is what I had been doing all these years: protecting my vulnerability by shutting others out emotionally. So many of these foster children did the same thing.

What I learned at this job helped me be there to help other children deal with the trauma and abuse they had endured at the hands of their parents. I wanted to "save" them while at the same time I was in a way saving myself through the work of helping others. It was a way for me to deal head-on with child abuse and face the reality of what I had gone through as a child with my father. This drive to save others made me good at my job. I took on a relatively heavy caseload but always made time to treat each child as an individual. My coworkers and my supervisor were always commenting on how dedicated and hardworking I was.

I will never forget one case, and it still haunts my dreams at night. When I read the case file, I was in awe that this was real and was not out of a horror film. I read: *One year old boy, bite marks on face, body and genitals, was dropped on pavement out of his stroller due to biological mother being intoxicated on several drugs. The boy had cerebral palsy due to this fall. He had not had any human affection. Does not know how to receive affection and fears everyone.*

Tears were streaming down my face as I was reading what I could not believe. How could a mother do this to her own child? I had to gather my emotions because nothing could prepare me for what was coming next. I had to go to the hospital to see this child and try to find placement in a proper foster home for him to live. I drove to the hospital thinking, *I can't imagine what this poor child has been through.* As I was walking through the hospital to the boy's room, my heart was racing. My hands were clammy, and I was so nervous about going into his room. I wanted to run. In my gut, I knew what I was about to see was going to change my life.

I stood in the doorway and saw a crib that looked like a jail cell. My eyes shifted to the bottom of the crib. I saw a child who looked as though he was a seven-month-old baby. He was so thin because he had been starved. He laid on his side staring into space. He had bite marks; there must have been fifty visible.

I was frozen and then I approached the crib. I leaned down so this sweet child could see safe eyes. Our eyes met and you could see he was curious who this woman was. I slowly took down the crib gate and I put my hand out. He was so terrified that he jumped, as if I was going to hurt him like the adults he'd come into contact before had hurt him. He'd never known a soft touch.

I slowly took his hand in mine and smiled as he let me hold his hand. I could not believe it. He smiled back. With a tear streaming down my cheek, I took this boy and held him in my arms. I walked with him in my arms to a rocking chair in the corner of the room by the window. I sat in the rocking chair with him and sang to him. He put his head back to meet my eyes. I looked under his chin.

In the case file it read the biological mother was so high that she thought she was eating food. His mother in a drug-induced state had bitten and eaten a chunk of her son's chin. She was eating bites of her own child's flesh, the flesh that she helped create and carried in her belly for nine months. When I held him in my arms, he felt love for the first time in his first year on this earth.

This boy needed so much time to heal and it would be months before he could leave the hospital due to all the abuse. I went to that hospital every day for months. I held this beautiful boy and sang to him until he would fall asleep. The beauty of this was as the days passed was, he was excited for my visits. He would sit up in his crib to greet me with a smile from ear to ear.

Sometime later I found an angel, a foster mom who was the perfect fit for this child who needed so much love and care. He was never supposed to walk or talk. This woman showed him so much love and gave him so much care. He eventually walked and talked; he was healed by a true miracle.

I think about this boy, now a grown man. Where he is now? Not a day goes by I don't think of him. I truly believe my purpose on this earth is to help heal the trauma of others. I always have had a gift with people. I stayed in this job in foster care from 1999–2004. Although the number of cases I had were many, I remember every single child. I am forever grateful that I was able to be a part of what I view as "saving their lives."

CHAPTER 6

MEN

—

When I was single living in the city of Chicago, I had many male companions. I had a way with men. I used them and rarely was vulnerable. I would go on dates and have surface conversation. The darkness I carried inside of me was too painful to discuss. I always asked more questions about them. This way it was a deflection so I would not have to talk a lot about myself.

In my early twenties, it was most often the case that I would get with self-absorbed young men who just wanted to have sex. They didn't care much about my emotions or inner deep thoughts. My friends did not know about my risky sexual behaviors. I would go on dates, sleep with the guy, and then not call them again. I was on to the next man who was of interest to me.

I would never discuss my dates with my friends. I was very secretive. They didn't ask about the dates because I did not tell them I was going. I kept my dating life separate from my friends when it came to going from one guy to the next.

The men were interested in me because I was not clingy and not wanting to have an intense romance. Many of the men I went out with all said the same thing, "All the women I date talk about a future and getting married."

I would say, "Well, I am defiantly not wanting to get married now." This always worked out in my favor.

One night, I went to an apartment building in Chicago, which was my best friend Lila's building. All the hottest young singles lived here, and I loved going to hang there. Lila and I would die laughing talking about our nights out clubbing, smoking cigs, and just being single, young women in a big city.

That evening the elevator opened and this tall, buggy eyed, nerdy, awkward guy started to talk to me, and I engaged in the conversation.

He looked at me and said, "Hey, my name is David. Do you live in the building?"

I said, "Oh no. I am just here visiting my friend, Lila."

David said, "Would you mind giving me your number? I would like to take you out some time."

I smiled and said, "Sure. Sounds good." I gave him my number and got off on Lila's floor.

This man was one of the guys I dated who was not good looking. This also was the one guy who broke my heart and sent me into such a deep depression. It was a new side of the darkness I did not know had existed before.

It was a whirlwind romance. After a month of dating, he brought me to Michigan for a three-day weekend of a lot of connection emotionally and intimacy, but mostly because he was so open with me. I was not emotionally vulnerable with him. I was drawn to his intense interest in me. He "swept me off my feet," or so I thought at the time. Looking back, it was really me wanting so badly to feel loved and not a real intimate emotional connection.

We had been dating for three months when David asked me to go on a trip with him to meet his whole family, to meet his stepmother and father in New York and The Hamptons, then to meet his brother and sister-in-law in Boston, and to meet his biological mother in Vermont.

They would give him the go ahead that I was "marriage material." I did not realize this guy was raised in New York City on Park Ave. So, this was really, "Is she from enough money?" At this time, I was twenty-five and a "hot mess." I smoked two packs of Marlboro Lights a day, had no money to my name, drove a piece of shit car, and lived in a horrendous apartment. What did I have going for me? Only my charming personality, being attractive, and my "gift of gab." Parents loved me, and I literally could talk to a wall.

I was not prepared for what was to come on this trip. We arrived in New York City on Park Ave. The cab pulled up to a beautiful building on a pristine tree-lined street. He opened the cab door for me to get out. We were greeted by the doorman and then took an elevator up to the top floor. David's dad owned the whole floor—the penthouse. I had never been to New York before, and I had no idea the amount of money people could have.

My mother always said, "You think someone has money. There is always someone with a lot more. Trust me." This comment from my mother did not make sense until that day.

The elevator door opened, and it was his front door. David had never discussed that his family came from old money. I looked at David and said, "Holy shit! This is insane!" (Really classy, huh?) I never did have a filter. The money I came from was literally nothing compared to David's family. I might as well have been homeless. His parents were at their other house in the Hamptons. We were going to meet them there tomorrow when we were rested.

I ran room to room in awe of the house that was a whole floor of an apartment building. It must have been over five thousand square feet. Beautiful paintings hung on the walls. Furniture was Art Deco. That was the coolest place I have still ever seen in my life. The next day we rented a car and drove to The Hamptons. I did not know what The Hamptons were. I did not have the attire to be there. I was a poor social worker.

When we arrived, the house was nothing short of spectacular. It was a mansion; everything was perfectly manicured on the outside. When the door opened his stepmother and father greeted us. His stepmother was about five-foot-three, thin, had a black bob and a very "New York" look. I remember thinking this woman is stone cold. She seemed to be judging me from the second she laid eyes on me.

"She is cute," David's stepmom said to him. I knew she meant in the sense "not rich enough cute." I could tell due to the tone of her voice and her facial expression when she said this.

His dad could not have been nicer. He was a short Jewish man, balding, with little glasses. We came out of the foyer and into the kitchen. Everything about this home was immaculate like a museum. I was quiet taking it all in. I did notice that this guy I had been dating, who previously had been Mr. Personality, all the sudden acted like a meek adolescent version of himself around his stepmother. She was not a kind woman. At every chance she would passively put him down.

David's stepmother said, "Drew, where did you grow up?"

I said, "The suburbs of Chicago."

"Where did you go to university? What do your mother and father do for a living? Where did they grow up? Where did they go to school for university? What do you do for a living? Where do you live?"

I continued to answer all her questions she was throwing at me as quickly as they were being asked hoping I was up to par for her test of me and my background.

It was the first-degree at its finest, and I was failing miserably. I knew I did not fit the bill for wealth in his family, but I could tell David's father had a soft spot for me. His demeanor and the way he spoke to me were gentle and kind. Even though he knew I would never marry his son because of my background, he seemed to like me as a person and enjoy my company.

We spent the next couple of days and nights going to lunches and dinners, all of which were very fancy and expensive. I felt stiff and uncomfortable in these environments. Even though I was raised going to nice restaurants, this was on a different level. Everyone in the restaurant was talking unusually quiet. This was not the scene I was used to. I did my best to acclimate to the restaurant and the continued questioning that occurred. I was on my most appropriate behavior. I only wanted to make a good impression on both of his parents.

Our next stop was Boston to meet David's sister-in-law and brother and their children. When we arrived, I could tell that David was embraced by his brother and his brother's family. They were warm to him and welcoming, and a sincerity was felt throughout the initial encounter that he had with them.

"This is quite a big deal that David brought you to meet his family. Could be something big like an engagement!" his sister-in-law said to me.

My eyes grew wide, and fear swept over me. I was not running to the altar any time soon. Unlike his wife, I could tell David's brother immediately did not care for me. He said, "Hello, nice to meet you." in a very cold manner. I was happy to meet their children. I had always been good with kids.

The way David acted around his brother and sister-in-law was like he was trying to impress them with his wit and dry humor. He was acting goofy and overcompensating, trying to be funny and get attention from his brother. David only wanted the good review of me from the older brother he idolized. He always spoke highly of his brother and how impressed he was with his brother's life and family.

During that visit, it became clear to me that his brother did not envision me as part of David's dream life. This is what David aspired to have one day: kids, a home, and a family. Let's say the stay was short and sweet. His brother ignored me 80 percent of the time I was there. I felt rejected and bad inside that this brother, who I had just met, judged me without even getting to know me.

We left David's brother's and drove to Vermont to meet his biological mother. David's mother was the warmest most open, welcoming woman I had met on this trip so far. She invited us in, and when she embraced him, he melted right into her arms. He was vulnerable, soft, silly, open, and kind just like she was. David loved his mother, and I could tell.

We sat with her in the kitchen, and she asked about me, my family, and my work. She was not asking to see if I fit the bill for her son but rather because she genuinely liked me as a person. I could always tell if someone cared for me or not within the first five minutes of meeting me. It is a gift and a curse, I always say.

I really liked this woman, and I could tell she had lived an incredible life. She was full of stories and experiences that made her the woman she was. David was so relaxed with his mother and was a whole different man than he had been with his brother, stepmother, and father. This was his authentic self.

We spent two days with her, and it was wonderful. When it was time for me to leave, I thanked her for her hospitality and told her how nice it had been to meet her. I left and David stayed back only to meet me back in Chicago in a couple of days. I was not prepared for what was to come when he returned to Chicago.

The night David came home, he called and asked to come over. I packed a bag to stay over at his place. I was so excited to see him. Also, I was dying to hear what his family had thought of me. He called saying he was outside. I ran to the front of my apartment building in Old Town Chicago with my sleepover bag in hand.

David looked at me and said, "I can no longer be with you anymore. We have to break up."

Before I could get a word out, David walked away from me, got into his car and drove away. I stood motionless, in shock of what had just happened. I thought, *Holy shit. He dumped me because of his family.*

I walked back into my apartment, dropped my bag to the ground, and fell and wept on the floor. I laid in a fetal position, rocking myself and crying so hard. I felt my heart had broken in half. In the days to come, I called in sick to work. I chained smoked and cried constantly.

One day when I had called in sick to work, it was pouring outside, and I called David from a payphone outside. I was hysterically crying, begging him to take me back.

"I am sorry. I can't do this right now. I am at work," he said and then he hung up.

I just stood there, the rain pummeling me. I walked back to my apartment and slept the rest of the day.

The days and months to come brought out depressive symptoms in me that I never knew were inside of me. I began to have symptoms of my first major depressive episode.

"A major depressive episode includes symptoms that are severe enough to cause noticeable difficulty in day-to-day activities. Such as work, school, social-activities or relationships."[20]

One night I was sitting on my couch listening to sad music, and for some reason I was holding a safety pin. I looked at it and thought, "Maybe if I scratch my skin with this, I could focus on the pain of that scratch instead of the pain in my heart." That was the day I began to cut. It started out with me taking the pin and making lines of scratches on my inner thighs. This way no one could see the scratches. I never had worn skirts or shorts; I always wore pants to work or jeans.

"For some people, when depression and anxiety lead to a tornado of emotions, they turn to self-harm looking for a release."[21]

In the days to come I would come home from work, smoke, listen to sad music, not answer my friends' or family's phone calls. I would sit and scratch my leg until it was bleeding. I was beginning to scare myself. The scratches all together looked very painful, and a huge scab began to form. This was becoming a dangerous habit. Every time I had the urge to cut, I took the pin and after I did it, I felt relief. It became a sick cycle.

My friends and I in the summer went to the rooftop pool of Lila's apartment building. I had forgotten about the cuts on my leg, but my friend immediately noticed them.

"Oh, my god! what the hell happened to your leg!"

"It was from when we were drunk. I fell and cut it," I lied.

She did not seem to believe me. "Are you cutting your leg?"

I looked her dead in the face. "That is insane. No." I dropped the subject. My heart was racing knowing she knew I was lying. I could not get the pain out of my heart from this breakup. The more I cut, the more I knew I was going to a dark place that I needed to get out of. I would continue to cut until one day I took it too far.

It was another night, alone in my apartment smoking, listening to music, the urge nudging me like a small child who wanted to play a game with you pulling on your shirt until you played. I thought, *I am going to get a knife.* The safety pin was not giving me the relief as it had in the past. I took a knife out of the kitchen drawer, and I sat on the floor. I put it on my arm. For the first time, I felt scared, like this is heavy shit that I must stop. I ended up putting the knife away. I would again have the relief of the safety pin.

Self-harm is never a good option. I could have used my healthy coping skills in many ways during my time of so much pain. I could have trusted a friend to talk about what I was going through at the time. Or I could have called a hotline to give me the support in my time of need. But I had not told a soul on earth I was hurting myself.

I also had not told one person I knew that I wanted to die. I began to have suicidal thoughts I wanted to end the pain in my broken heart. I did not have a plan of how I was going to kill myself. I just kept thinking; *I don't want to be here anymore.*

I worked in the field of Social Work. I knew once I admitted to wanting to die, I would go into a hospital. I was smart. I never would let myself go there. I needed to survive. I kept the darkness inside of me. It was like no pain I could ever explain. The only way to explain this darkness inside of me it was like the dementors in *Harry Potter* sucking the happiness out of my soul. It felt like I was in a dark hole of blackness, like I had been looking up from the bottom of that hole and could not escape.

Every time I have felt I do not want to be here anymore; I always remind myself that I am a Weeble. This was a plastic toy we played with when I was growing up in the seventies as a small child. When you hit the toy, it bounced right back up, no matter how hard you tried to knock it down. I was going to Weeble and I always did… Of course, the day I finally came out of my darkness was the day that motherfucker called me to talk.

Isn't that how it always works? Like men have a radar, "Ok sir she is healed now. It is time to remind her that you miss her."

I picked up the phone and David said, "Hey, I have been thinking about you."

"Oh really, and what have you been thinking about?"

"Well, I saw a car that looked like yours on the street and I was wondering how you were doing and if you wanted to get together some night?"

"Maybe. I must see. I have been busy at work. I have to go."

"Ok then, nice to talk to you."

"Bye." I hung up not believing after all this time, six months later, I felt sad, but the darkness had lifted inside of me. I would end up meeting David for a drink a week after his call. It was awkward and quiet. After seeing him that night, I did not see him again. I was finally over David.

Ironically, he lives in the suburb next to the one I currently live in. When I have seen him, when I am running an errand, I always remember what happened and it makes me very sad. Not sad because I did not end up with this person.

I get sad because I allowed a man to make me feel broken, as if I had nothing to live for. It taught me that no matter how bad things feel at the time, time heals everything. Suicide and self-harm are not the answers when a person is in pain. Time heals all emotional wounds, even the ones that feel like they can never be healed.

If you ever feel these dark thoughts, I'm here to tell you that you are worth living for because life is better with you in it. I am living proof that there is light at the end of a dark tunnel that seems hopeless. I am grateful I choose to no longer self-harm and I know that suicide is never an option.

When you feel that the darkness inside of you is too much to handle, it is always helpful to reach out for support, so you are not alone. There is always another option rather than self-harming. Reaching out for help is a sign of strength, not a sign of weakness.

The National Suicide Prevention Lifeline provides twenty-four-seven support. The number to call is 1-800-273-8255. If I knew this help line existed at the time, I was going through this breakup I would have used it myself. Another helpful resource is the crisis text line. A crisis counselor for self-harm can be reached at 741741 or you can use the mobile click to text button on crisistextline. org. Another resource for help when battling thoughts of self-harm number is 1-800-448-3000 or www.your-lifeyourvoice.org/email: Text VOICE to 20121

CHAPTER 7

SOULMATE

———

When I was twenty-six, I was not the girl looking at wedding magazines like all my friends were. While my friends gushed over big white gowns, talking about how big their diamond engagement rings would be, I rolled my eyes and said, "I am in no rush at all to get married like all of you are."

I was looking at fashion magazines and reading *US Weekly* instead. I hated the whole idea of a wedding. I was happy with dating and the freedom I had being single in the city. I felt no pressure to conform and become a housewife any time soon. I did not believe "the one" existed for me to marry. Until I met him.

I truly feel life is full circle. The man I would end up marrying was someone I had grown up with. Tyler was one year older than me in school. We attended the same high school. I always thought Tyler was hot, and I would say hi to him in the hallways in between classes. We also went to the same parties on weekends. Tyler knew who I was because my older sister Devon had a class with him. Everyone I grew up with knew Tyler. My friends and I hung out with his guy friends on the weekends. Tyler spent most of the time with his girl-friend, Andy, who was in my grade. When he graduated high school, I did not see Tyler again until I was twenty-six.

One night I decided to go out with my friend Karen to a bar called Joe's. We were sitting in a booth when a man in a suit said, "Hey, so great to see you!"

I could not believe it. It was Tyler from high school. He was just as gorgeous as the last time I had seen him all those years ago. Tyler had blue piercing eyes, dark hair, a nice build, and smelled good. I get weak when a man smells good. I noticed that he had so much confidence. I was always a sucker for confidence. I always found it so attractive when a man could hold his own.

Little did I know Tyler was on a date with a girl I was acquainted with. She was sitting at a table and did not see who Tyler was talking to. I didn't say anything to her because I wanted to talk to Tyler. "Can I have your phone number? I would love to take you out some night," Tyler asked.

I smiled at him. "Sure. Here is my number." I took the napkin that was on our table, asked the waitress for a pen, and wrote my phone number down and handed it to Tyler.

He smiled and said, "Thanks. I will talk to you soon."

"Talk to you soon."

Karen and I looked at one another and she smiled. "That is the guy you are going to marry."

"Shut up. You're ridiculous!" We both laughed, drank, and talked the rest of that night.

A week later, I received a call from Tyler. What he didn't know was that I had just gone on the worst date the night before. A friend of mine had set me up with a guy named Dan who she had met at East Bank Club. East Bank was a prestigious health club in Chicago. My friend knew a lot of people there and she felt we would have a good time together. So, when Dan called me, I did not hesitate to say yes.

I met up with Dan at a coffee shop. He looked like a model out of a magazine. Tall, perfect body, nice eyes, gorgeous hair, dressed in jeans, a tee shirt that fit him perfectly, and cool sneakers. I thought, *Well done! This guy is a twelve out of ten*!

From the get-go Dan and I had so much sexual chemistry. You could cut it with a knife. Dan leaned over as I was in mid-sentence and started kissing me. He had great looks, confidence, was sexy, and was aggressive in a good way. I was sold and kissed him back. Thinking back, it was a bold move. I had just met Dan a half hour before. This intense make-out session was in front of everyone at the coffee shop, but I honestly did not care at the time. I was young and in the moment. I felt it was safe, so I went with it. I was also never one to turn down intense sexual chemistry.

Dan asked if I wanted to go somewhere else and I agreed, thinking we would be going to a lounge or a restaurant. We walked to Dan's car, and he drove to what I realized was a parking garage.

"Where are you going? Why are we here?"

Dan stopped the car and put it in park. I heard the sub-conscious voice again, *"Run!"* I could not run the doors were locked.

I calmly said, "Dan, I have a headache can you please drive me home?" Dan proceeded to lean over and stick his tongue in my mouth. He crawled over to my side and was trying to get on top of me.

At that moment, I thought I was going to be raped. Just like the ongoing story of my life, no one was there to save me. No one to validate what was happening to me. Just me and another layer of trauma.

I screamed, "Get off me! Please, take me home!" Dan was not pleased but he got off me and drove me home. I thanked g-d that night for looking after me. That was the closest to rape I had ever been, and it was terrifying. I never saw or talked to Dan again after our date.

The day after my terrifying date Tyler called. I lied, and said, "I am so sorry I can't make it to our date. My mother has a migraine and I have to take care of her."

Tyler said, "I hope she feels better. I will call you again to reschedule."

"Sounds good. I will talk to you soon." I hung up and felt so bad for lying. I just was still shaking from what had happened with Dan the night before.

Later, I found out from Tyler that he planned a romantic date that night that I canceled. He made reservations to a nice dinner, bought me flowers, the whole nine yards.

Weeks passed and I was working at my desk. I always was in the field when I worked in foster care. I was rarely at my desk but this one day I was catching up on paperwork when my phone rang. It was Tyler.

"Hey, remember me? What do you think of us trying for another date?"

"Yes, that sounds great! You can pick me up at 7:30 p.m."

"Sounds good. I will see you later."

"See you later. I'm looking forward to it." I hung up the phone really excited for our date. I was so happy that he had called me again to go out.

Tyler picked me up that night at 7:30 p.m. I wore jeans, a long sleeve black tight shirt, and minimal makeup. I felt sexy and confident, and I was so ready to go on our date. I walked down to his car.

"You look really pretty," Tyler said when he saw me.

I smiled and said, "Thank you. You look nice too." I walked around to the other side of the car. Tyler followed me and opened my door for me. He was a real gentleman; not many guys were door openers when you would get in their cars.

Tyler made a reservation at a nice sushi restaurant. We were seated at our table and Tyler pulled out my chair for me. I sat down and the conversation flowed. I did not skirt around the questions he was asking. For the first time, I allowed myself to feel vulnerable. I felt it was safe to share with Tyler. I wanted to share what I thought about the topics he was asking. I had never done that on any other dates I had gone on. And I had gone on too many to count. I knew this was something special. We talked for hours about everything: our families, passions, jobs, friends, and past relationships.

Tyler asked me the important questions that I never allowed guys to ask.

"Do you see yourself married with kids?"

"Yes, I do actually. I just am not running to the altar. I have never thought about it seriously."

"Well, maybe you just haven't met the right person yet," he said this with a smirk on his face.

I smiled and replied, "Well, maybe not. You never know."

I remember thinking on this date, *this guy is my soul mate.*

When we finished dinner, Tyler paid the bill and we walked outside. As we waited for the valet to bring the car, Tyler looked at me with those blue piercing eyes and then leaned in for the most gentle, romantic, and soft sensual kiss. He put his hand on my face behind my ear and pulled me toward him. His other hand was around my waist. I kissed him back as if I was melting into him. This feeling when I was kissing Tyler was the warmth, I was so familiar with. Believe me, I had kissed half the city of Chicago at this point in my life. But the feeling was also different because it was not just sexual. It was emotional. For me this was always a danger zone because I guarded my heart. I knew this man was going to guard my heart just as I had been doing for myself all this time. It was that deep our connection and we both knew this was something special.

"I had a really great time tonight. I would like to take you out again," he said.

"I had a great time too; I would love to go out with you again."

After our date, Tyler drove me to my place. He got out of the car and opened my car door for me; it was very "old school." He walked me to the front door of my building and said, "Goodnight."

He kissed me again and I asked him to come up. I was planning on sleeping with him. He said, "All we have is time, and I want to take it slow."

Slow was not in my dating vocabulary. "Well, that is a first. You don't want to come up?"

He smirked. "I want to, but I am not going to."

I knew this guy was the one. He respected me as a woman and as a person. I liked that about him.

We continued to date and spend almost every waking hour with one another. When we were not working, I would spend the night at his place, or he would stay at mine. A month later, Tyler asked me when we were at his place, "Drew, will you move in with me?"

I was surprised and shocked, "Are you serious? You know if I say yes and you break up with me, you have to buy me all new furniture."

He laughed at that. "I am never breaking up with you."

We moved into a three-bedroom, two-bathroom condo. It was beautiful, hardwood floors, granite countertops everywhere. Pure luxury compared to how I had been living all of those years single in the city. It was honestly pure luxury—period. The location was amazing; I was truly living my dream.

Three months passed and Tyler asked me if I would go with him to The Peninsula Hotel in the city.

"Tyler, why are we going there? That is so nice."

"Get dressed. I want to take you out."

A couple of hours later I was dressed and ready to go. I noticed Tyler was nervous. He was fidgety and looked like he was sweating. His mind was in another place.

I asked him, "Are you okay? What's up with you?"

He responded with a smile. "Nothing. I am just happy to be with you tonight."

In my gut, I knew he was going to propose to me that evening. I also saw the ring box in the pocket of his pants. I did not say anything about it because I was overwhelmed of what was to come that night. I thought how all this time being a single woman I never thought this would be me being proposed to. I felt excited and nervous at the same time. I knew my life was going to drastically change. It was also comforting knowing that this man I loved so deeply was going to ask me to be with him forever; to me that meant everything. I was so grateful he came into my life when he did. All the dysfunction I'd had before Tyler I could now put behind me and start anew.

We pulled up to the hotel. Tyler opened the car door for me. I got out and he took my hand in his while smiling.

"We are going to go to the bar to have some drinks."

I smiled and said, "Let's go."

We sat for a while talking when Tyler got up from his seat. He got down on one knee. "Drew, will you marry me?"

With tears in my eyes, I looked at him without hesitation and said, "Yes, I will."

He put a beautiful engagement ring on my finger. It was a one carat diamond with two diamond baguettes on the sides. Diamonds surrounded the whole band. It was perfect. We kissed and celebrated that we were now engaged. The people in the bar cheered with excitement that they had just witnessed an engagement. It was such a night to remember.

The next week I talked to my father about how I just got engaged. I asked him to pick me up so we could go for coffee and talk about the wedding. In the car on the way to the coffee shop, I said, "Dad, I want you to sit at the head table with Tyler and me."

"Is your mother at the head table?" My parents were divorced, and they did not speak. "Drew, I am not sitting at the head table with your mother."

"Dad, please can you sit there? The seating chart is full, we would like you to sit with us."

My father stared at me shocked. "Drew, I am not going to your wedding. I am not walking you down the aisle. Get the fuck out of my car!"

With tears in my eyes, I got out of my father's car. I was in disbelief at what just had happened. I called Tyler on my cell phone and told him what happened and asked him if he could pick me up. Within ten minutes, Tyler was there to get me. I was sobbing. I felt so betrayed that my father would not be coming to our wedding.

Tyler comforted me, saying, "Drew, it will be okay because we will be together. I will always be here for you as long as I live."

"I love you. Thank you for always being there."

I did not hear from my father again after that encounter in the car.

We married eight months later May 10, 2004; in the suburb I grew up in. I'd hated the wedding planning. The whole process really did not interest me. I was mostly looking forward to the honeymoon in Aruba. As my father had promised he did not show up at my wedding. On my wedding day, I wore a white strapless beautiful wedding gown. I had my makeup done but did my own hair. I had a short straight bob at the time with side swept bangs. I was glowing, and I was so excited to marry Tyler.

The room we were going to get married in was filled with pink peonies. There was a white chuppah, which is a canopy under which a Jewish couple stand during the wedding ceremony. It consists of cloths or sheet, stretched or supported over four poles, and it symbolizes the home the couple will build together. On both sides of the room were chairs that would seat 120 guests. The aisle was white and stretched from the beginning of the room to where the chuppah stood. Lining the aisle were candles lit in little votives and mid-size votives.

It's a room out of a wedding magazine, I thought.

The ceremony began and my bridesmaids and Tyler's groomsmen walked down the aisle. They departed on each side and Tyler walked down the aisle with his parents. Then the music began for me. It was Pachelbel's Canon in D. As the classical music played, my whole single life flashed before my eyes. My mother waited for me as I walked through the door. All our guests turned around to see me. I was overwhelmed and cried. I could not believe this was my wedding. It felt like a surreal dream that I was walking into. I looked at the room filled with our family and friends. I took my mother's arm as she walked me down the aisle.

I saw Tyler waiting for me at the end with a huge proud smile on his face. When I reached him, he put out his hand. I took it and the ceremony began. It was a traditional Jewish ceremony and lasted about an hour. The traditional prayers for the bride and groom were said. We drank wine and then I put Tyler's wedding band on with a prayer and he put my band on my finger with a prayer and we kissed. Before the ceremony ended, we enacted the Jewish tradition of stepping on glass in a cloth, which represents the destruction of the Temple in Jerusalem. Hand in hand we walked down the aisle as man and wife.

It was one of the best days of my life.

CHAPTER 8

KIDS

—

That first year, I found myself envisioning having a family, and I eventually worked up the courage to tell Tyler what I wanted. One day I was in the shower. Tyler was in the bathroom shaving and getting ready for work.

"I think we should have a baby."

Tyler smiled ear to ear and said, "Let's do it. Let's have a baby."

On our first try we conceived. I chose to quit my job in foster care, and I decided that I was going to be a stay-at-home mom. I was not upset about not working anymore. I was ready for the next phase of my life to begin. I felt I had done a good job working in foster care and now it was time to have my own family. My pregnancy was tough. I had morning sickness constantly. I felt hungry, almost starving, all the time, and I would sit on the couch watching TV and eating endless amounts of powdered donuts. They were my absolute favorite. I gained forty-six pounds by the end of the nine months.

Tyler and I were in the grocery store the night before I was to be induced to have our baby girl. I grabbed a package of powdered donuts and Tyler said, "I think you have had enough of those." This is one thing any smart man knows not to say to a huge pregnant woman.

I gave Tyler a death stare. "Well, I guess my powered donut days are over."

We laughed and left the grocery store.

The next day was May 7, 2005, the day our daughter Madison was brought into the world. I had a very long labor that lasted about fourteen hours. I was exhausted, and I had not slept much the night before because I was anticipating the next day. After the brutal delivery I was given Madison to hold. I looked at her in awe of what Tyler and I had created. She was perfect. Before she was born, I didn't realize the amount of instant love I would feel for this child.

Being a mother came naturally to me. I never had a night nurse or babysitters except for my own mother and my mother-in-law. I wanted Tyler and me to do this on our own. Tyler was amazing as a new father, and we took turns in the middle of the night to bottle feed Madison. Tyler never once complained about getting up. He fed her and sang to her; it was adorable.

Madison was not an easy baby as she had colic the first three months. She cried all the time. It was hard and exhausting. I started to feel like a walking zombie. I was getting up every hour on the hour to feed and take care of Madison.

One night at two in the morning, I was bottle feeding her. I must have dozed off for a moment because when I woke up, I noticed the bottle was in her ear. I could not believe how exhausted I was every day and night. During the day when Madison would nap, I would also take a nap to try to catch up on all the lost sleep that I needed so desperately. I just went with it because I was so grateful for her. I realized how lucky Tyler and I were to have had a healthy baby. At the time, I had so many girlfriends who were struggling to get pregnant and doing IVF to have their own children.

A year into us living in our downtown condo Tyler and I decided we would be better off raising a family in the suburbs so we bought our first home in the suburbs of Chicago. We decided to move to the suburbs so our children would have a yard to play in. It was a twelve-hundred-square-foot starter home. It had two small bedrooms and one and a half bathrooms. It was a bi-level home with a detached garage.

When Madison was two years old Tyler asked me if we could try for a second child. I was hesitant at first. I did not know if I could manage two children. Tyler said to me, "Drew, Madison needs a friend. We can't just have one child."

It took some convincing for me to agree to having second child. In the back of my mind, I was fearful of getting postpartum depression. I don't know why; I just had a gut feeling that I would get it after I had a second baby. I finally agreed though. "Let's do it. Let's have another baby."

It did not take long until I got pregnant again. At our five-month doctor appointment, Tyler and I found out we would be having another daughter. I was excited. I knew Madison having a sister would be so great for her and for us.

My second pregnancy was easy compared to the first, but I still had some morning sickness. This time around I knew what to expect being pregnant. This pregnancy I was not craving powdered donuts and instead I was craving fruit and lox sandwiches. I also ate much healthier than during the first pregnancy and it made a big difference; I only gained twenty-eight pounds with the second pregnancy. I felt less weighted down.

I went in to be induced at the hospital with our second daughter. The delivery was quick and easy compared to the first. Sara came into the world on April 27, 2008. She was calm and beautiful. Sara slept well and was not fussy, and everything came easily with her. Sara smiled at four weeks.

Having two kids was way harder than just one. She never gave me a hard time but even so, when we brought Sara home, having two children was a lot for me to handle, especially since Tyler went to work full time. I stayed home with both kids, and I felt overwhelmed. I had to make sure that Madison who was a toddler was getting enough attention and love while also tending to a newborn baby who constantly needed her diapers changed and needed to be held and fed. I also had to make sure she was getting enough stimulation for her growth mentally. This was not an easy feat for any new mother. It was like a balancing act and every day I had to make sure both girls were well taken care of.

I loved them both so much.

Six months to the day after Sara was born Tyler told me one weekend day to go to the mall to relax and walk around. He always was an amazing help with the girls. He was thoughtful when it came time for me to take a break.

"Thank you so much. I really needed some alone time," I told him.

I got into our Jeep and then kissed Tyler and the girls good-bye. I turned on the radio. I was halfway to the mall when a feeling like a black cloud surrounded my thoughts and feelings. It felt like an overwhelming emotion of sadness that I could not control inside of myself. I began to cry, and I suddenly thought, *I am going to either drive my car into a tree or drive off the overpass.* I was having symptoms of post-partum depression. Postpartum depression is common as "approximately 70–80 percent of women will experience, at a minimum, the baby blues. Many of these women will experience the more severe condition postpartum depression."[22]

There is a shift in mood, sleep pattern, anxiety level and the person experiencing these symptoms feels like "something is off."[23] Leading up to the day I was having irritability, insomnia, was crying a lot and felt depressed. I had difficulty concentrating, and I was having a hard time with the daily activities of being a new mother. All these factors were red flags of symptoms of postpartum depression.

At the time, though, I had no idea what was going on. I felt as if my emotions and thoughts were in chaos. I was just set on ending my life. I picked up the cell phone crying hysterically and called my mother.

"Mom, I am going to drive my car into a tree or drive off an overpass."

My mom sounded panicked and confused. "What is going on? What is happening? Why are you feeling this way?"

I just responded, "I want to die."

My mother talked to me all the way home. Before I walked into the house, I told my mom I was going to talk to Tyler.

When I walked into the house, I was hysterical. "I want to die," I said, tears streaming down my face.

Tyler looked at me, not understanding how I had gone from happy just an hour before to this intense emotion of sadness. I told Tyler that I thought it would be a good idea to go to the hospital to see what they said.

We walked in and I just sobbed thinking, *I cannot be committed to the psych ward. This is not going to happen on my watch.*

We were brought back to the ER and a social worker came in, asking me all sorts of questions about my mental state. As a mental health worker, myself, I knew what she was going to ask me, and I was very careful about how I answered her questions. I knew what to say and what not to say in the assessment. It felt very strange to be on the other side of the questions and not the person asking them. I felt vulnerable and scared and I had my guard up.

When she left the room I told Tyler, "I will not be committed here. Let's make a plan where I cannot be left alone." He agreed and I was not committed. I told the ER social worker that I would go to a partial program at the hospital to get medication to deal with the depression. I would also go to groups for emotional support during this time.

When I went back home, I was not functional, and I cried all the time. I could not care for the girls fully. Tyler was my rock, and his parents, my mother, sisters, and cousin all were there to help. I told Tyler one evening that I was going to take a bath. I started to feel a familiar feeling. The tugging, the pull to cut myself to release the intense pain inside. I went to the cabinet and there it was. My old friend the safety pin. I took out the pin and I began to cut my leg in the bath. I felt that relief I had felt before. I felt the blood trickle down my leg into the bath water, and I heard, "Are you okay in there?"

I replied, "Yes," with a rush of disgust and guilt inside of me. I never told Tyler that I had cut myself that day. That was the only time during my postpartum that I had done that. I knew I could not start to self-harm again. I was a mother now with two kids and a husband who needed me. I had to work through the uncomfortable feelings of sadness, hopelessness, and depression.

After the first month I felt a little better and was hopeful I could move forward beyond the postpartum depression. I noticed things getting better and better each week, if I kept fully participating in therapy. I met with a therapist weekly, went to groups, took medication and I finally came out of the darkness. I had the constant support from Tyler, my mother, sisters, and cousins during this time. They helped with the girls every day and drove to get my prescriptions if I needed them when Tyler was at work.

It was a process and I had to take it day by day but ultimately the immersive therapy, my hard work, and the support from my loved ones helped me come out of the darkness and into the light.

CHAPTER 9

WORK BEGINS

Before I turned thirty, I was not yet ready to get an assessment or receive a diagnosis. I had always avoided getting a mental health assessment up until this point. It felt very different when I turned thirty. It was time for me to accept that what had happened to me was not my fault. I was ready to face what I was so afraid of and begin the journey to emotional healing. I was a mother and I wanted to be the best I could be emotionally for the girls, Tyler, and for me.

I did not ask for the abuse that had happened to me to create this chemical imbalance in my brain. I felt a turning point when it came to my mental health as I had been through so many ups and downs in my life. I wanted to feel balanced. It was time for me to take control of how I felt and finally reach out for the help I needed.

I went to a psychologist and asked if she could give me an assessment to find out my diagnosis. I felt nervous and unsure. I was afraid that if I had a diagnosis, it would make me feel like I was "crazy." I did not want to be labeled like something was wrong with me.

During the assessment, the doctor asked me questions about my thoughts, feelings, and behaviors. This was part of my mental health history. She asked me how these affected my everyday life, and which made them better or worse. She was also observing my appearance and behavior to see if I was having anxiety or if I was experiencing any symptoms during the assessment.

She asked me simple questions regarding my everyday schedule and how I cared for myself and my family. This was the personal history part of the assessment. I was asked about my family history regarding any mental illness on my mother or father's side of the family. If I ever had any hospitalizations and how long, I have had symptoms. If I was married, if I worked, what my upbringing was like and what my major traumatic experiences I'd had in my life.

The next part of the assessment was the cognitive evaluation. I was asked questions about recalling information and using mental reasoning. The assessment lasted an hour and a half.

After I had an assessment, the doctor told me I had a diagnosis of Bipolar two Disorder. The diagnosis felt like it fit for me given the thoughts, feelings, and behaviors I'd had my whole life. It felt like the missing piece of the puzzle that I had been searching for was finally found. The feelings of hypomania and depression no longer felt like a mystery.

Now it was time to get a treatment plan to deal with my diagnosis in a healthy way. I started weekly therapy with a new therapist I had found after going to the program at the hospital when I had post-partum depression. I also began to go to a new psychiatrist who put me on medication to balance my moods. I had facts and the right treatment team to help me feel better.

As part of my treatment plan, my therapist recommended Dialectical Behavioral Therapy, also known as DBT therapy. Dialectical Behavioral therapy is an evidence-based psychotherapy that can be useful in treating mood disorders, suicidal ideation, and for change in behavioral patterns such as self-harm, and substance abuse.[24]

The whole purpose of this therapy is for the individual to take a situation, look at how they feel, and react to the situation. Then they use skills that they are taught to change the outcome of the situation. I expressed to my therapist that I was open to any new therapeutic ideas to help in my recovery process.

The first group I attended was held on a Wednesday night at 7:00 p.m. My hands were sweating, and my face felt flushed red, I was so nervous not knowing what to expect. As I climbed the stairs of the three-story brick building, I wondered what the people in the group would be like. I got to the third floor, opened the glass door, and there was a waiting room with two other people waiting to get into the group. We sat quietly until a man came out of the room and asked us to come back to start the group.

In the room, we found a circle of chairs with seven people already in them, both men and women. Their ages ranged from early twenties to late fifties. I felt uncomfortable, anxious, and quiet. I smiled when I walked in, trying not to make eye contact with anyone as I quietly sat down.

The leader of the group's name was Robert. He was a tall, slender man with white and grey hair in his fifties with urban style and nice round glasses. He began the group by handing out a notebook that read "DBT Skills" on the front of it. Robert explained to the group that this was a once-a-week, year-long course that would be held every Wednesday night at 7 p.m. Robert asked everyone in the circle to go around and introduce themselves. When it was my turn to introduce myself, I was so nervous.

"Hi. My name is Drew, and I am looking forward to learning the skills taught in this group." I smiled nervously at everyone else in the circle.

Robert said, "Thanks, Drew. We are happy to have you with us each week."

I was open to the fact I was going to learn something through this process. I was also opened to being vulnerable and sharing my experiences. I wanted to have a new beginning in my life to mend the past. I wanted to learn the healthy coping skills in this group to move forward into my recovery process.

I went every week religiously and did not skip one group. I shared my thoughts, experiences and feelings each week, absolutely committed to working on the DBT skills. I was noticing a difference in how I was viewing situations and the coping skills I was using to deal with each of them. One important skill was the use of diary cards. Robert gave everyone diary cards, which were on a piece of sturdy paper that had columns. On the top of the paper it read, SITUA-TION THAT TRIGGERED THE EMOTION. The middle column read THE EMOTIONS FELT THAT CAME WITH THE EXPERIENCE. The next column read HOW DID YOU HANDLE THE SITUATION. The last column was WHAT SKILLS DID YOU USE IN THIS SITUATION.

This diary card became like the "behavior bible" to the group. Each week we would go around the circle and discuss how we dealt with the week's distressing situations. Hearing everyone in the group and their independent experiences helped me tremendously. I no longer felt alone in my thoughts and feelings because the people in the group were having the same reactions as me. I was healing, and it was changing the way I dealt with my mental health.

I underwent such a transformation. My behaviors and thoughts about certain situations in my life changed. When my family triggered me, instead of lashing out, I would take out the diary card from my group and write down the specific example of what was said to me. If a friend or family member said something that would usually make me angry, I would write what emotions this made me feel and then I would take two skills, such as wise mind- "Wise mind is the perfect balance between reason and emotion."[25]

I took a pause before responding to my friend or family member. My family did not know I was using these skills as I was using them. I was using the DBT skills I learned and handling the situation differently. Then in turn I would get a better outcome, one without fighting. I sorted my reactions and avoided conflict. It was a more peaceful way of dealing for me.

I also was going to individual therapy with Robert each week. He would help me process what I was learning in the group. We would also talk about my family, husband and our relationship, and how I was managing with my girls. After a year in the group, I graduated with a certificate at the end of 2011. I was very proud of this accomplishment. I try to use the skills I had learned from DBT to this day.

During this therapy group I also got to know others with many disorders who had great functioning lives. Seeing others who struggled but still had functioning lives gave me hope. It made me feel less "crazy" and more "normal," whatever that means. But let's be honest. Who would really want to be normal? I mean just look at those people. Bo-ring!

Before this group I felt alone in my symptoms, that no one understood what I dealt with every day. Now I felt as if I had so much support and understanding when it came to my illness and my symptoms. I am so grateful that I was a part of this DBT group therapy.

Even with the intensive DBT group that year, I have still struggled at times with how my thoughts and feelings impact my relationships. Through the years, my relationships have suffered due to my ups and downs. My therapist says I am in a constant state of "trauma mind." My brain has never been healed from the suffering of the mental and physical abuse that I grew up with from my father. I have had many issues from being in this trauma state of mind including flashbacks, self-blame, panic attacks, hyper-arousal meaning high energy, sleep problems, and low self-esteem. I have had issues with feeling validation, which makes me feel not settled.

I have been to many therapists and psychiatrists throughout my life. I have never been on the right medication for my symptoms. I started taking Prozac when I was in my thirties. It seemed to help the depression at the time but really did not help the hypomania.

About five years after I participated in Dialectical Behavior Therapy, we were preparing for my oldest daughter to have a Bat Mitzvah, the rite of passage for a young Jewish girl at the age of thirteen. I had a debilitating fear of entertaining, which went back to my issues with having attention on me. It made me feel so much anxiety that I felt like I could barely breath. My older sister Devon was a fabulous entertainer. She had a business and she made invitations when she was in her twenties; she always knew how to put things together.

I was going to hire a planner for this event to take the stress off my husband and me. Devon insisted that she make the invitations and help plan the luncheon after the service. She also wanted to help plan the party for the adults and kids. I had a gut feeling this was not going to end well.

Devon may be a good planner, but she is a last-minute planner. I am a year in advance kind of planner. I get somewhere ten to twenty minutes early. Devon is usually late. This was a recipe for disaster, and that is an understatement. Since it had been so long since I had been in the Dialectical Behavior

Therapy group, my skills were rusty to say the least and not at the forefront of my mind. It was difficult to regulate my emotions like I had when I was in the group, and I wished I could have used them during this time when I needed them most.

The invitations were done, and Devon asked me to pick them up and stuff the envelopes. All the sudden I could feel it, the intense anxiety and irritability creeping up. I said to Devon, "Are you going to help me with this? What if I screw it up?"

She said, "I did the invites. Now you have to do this part."

I lost it. I literally was having a melt down inside. This was the beginning of an actual nervous breakdown. I stuffed the invites as best as I could and mailed them all out.

Just as I expected it was a mess. People were getting invites that were not theirs and there were missing invites in certain envelopes. The calls started to come in and I lost my shit at Devon. I yelled and screamed about how could she do this to me, but I had done this to myself. This was my issue not hers; she was just trying to be a helpful sister and do what she did best planning for entertaining people. I do believe if I had been going to the DBT group during this time I would have managed my emotions much better.

I felt so bad that I could not articulate to her I appreciated all her effort and help with the event. I did not have the proper skills to make it better when I so desperately wanted to. I was desperate to find a psychiatrist who could "cure" me. The medication that I was on was not effective when it came to my depression and hypomania. I was still easily triggered and could not manage my ongoing anxiety. I wanted a medication to fix the imbalance of my irritability and anxiety.

I found a doctor in the suburb I was living in at the time. I should have known by the reviews this man was a stone-cold con artist. I told Tyler that this doctor did not take insurance. Tyler was so worried about me. "Do what you have to. We will pay for it."

During my first call to the doctor, he sounded "very concerned." He seemed overly willing to help me.

When I went in, he asked me all about my childhood and laid out his plan for my treatment. "I am going to give you mini doses of medications and we are going to see how you react to them."

I had told the doctor that I was very sensitive to medications and was nervous about the side effects. He "reassured" me that I could call him when I was experiencing any major side effects. Little did I know at the time, because he failed to mention, that every time I would call him, he charged me $115.00 for just five to ten minutes of talking.

Our initial meeting was $500.00. At this point, I was willing to pay a million dollars just to fix my brain. In the two months that followed, this doctor took me for a whirlwind of a ride with the medications he prescribed.

The first thing he prescribed was Trileptal, which resulted in nauseated and flu-like symptoms. Trileptal "is an anticonvulsant or anti-epileptic medication. (I do not have epilepsy.) It works by decreasing nerve impulses that cause seizures and pain."[26] I called the doctor and he told me to stop taking the Trileptal and filled a new prescription for Depakote.

I said to the doctor, "I am feeling so sick I have horrible nausea and body aches and chills."

"Get off the Trileptal immediately and we will start you on Depakote."

"Do you think it is a good idea for me to take another medication before this medication is out of my system?"

"It is fine. Just follow my instructions."

I was hesitant and had a bad feeling about mixing medications, but I trusted this doctor, so I continued to follow his orders that he gave me.

Depakote "is used to treat various types of seizure disorders."[27] I had never experienced a seizure in my life. When I was on Depakote I was zoned out, sick and nauseated, and had tremors. I called the doctor after a day, and he told me to no longer take this medication and he would fill a prescription for Lamictal.

Lamictal "is used to delay mood episodes in adults with bipolar disorder."[28] When I was on Lamictal I felt irritable and zoned out like a zombie with my mind felt foggy. Once again, I called the doctor and he told me to discontinue the medication and he then prescribed me Topamax.

Topamax "is used to prevent migraine headaches."[29] I was having mood stability issues, not migraines. But I did not question the doctor because I trusted his process. With the Topamax he instructed me to open the capsule and take one to two grains every morning. I followed his instructions and did not feel sick, but it did not help the depression or hypomania.

The doctor told me to discontinue the medication. The next thing he put me on was Zyprexa which "is used to treat psychotic conditions such as schizophrenia and bipolar disorder."[30] I had another bad reaction, and the medication was making me vomit. The doctor told me to discontinue the medication and he prescribed me Lexapro which "is an antidepressant used to treat anxiety and major depression."[31]

At the time I was in such mental agony that I was willing to do anything to ease my symptoms. Honestly, I was desperate and would do anything to try and fix my brain's functioning. At the same time, I felt very angry and frustrated that I continued to take all these different medications without any of them working.

He put me on Lexapro before the prior medications were out of my system. This led to the darkness within me creeping in again, but this was not like when I had postpartum depression. The feeling I had with postpartum was depression with the feeling of hopelessness and fear of being a mother of two children.

I had more of an awareness about my feelings when I had postpartum and I did not feel numb, as I did while on this cocktail of medications. This time it felt like something was taking away all my happiness and will to live. I was on this medicine for two days, and every day I thought about death. I kept repeating to myself, "It is the medication not you. This is the medication not you."

Death is never an option nor should be when you are feeling that there is no way out. When I was on this medicine, the chemicals in my brain were telling me otherwise. I felt as if I was in a paralyzed state of mind and did not call the doctor right away. The second day I decided I needed fresh air and went for a walk. I told Tyler I would be back, but he could tell something was off with me due to the medications I had been taking.

"Drew, I don't trust this doctor. The medicines you have taken are not working."

"Just give it time he will find something that works."

Tyler said, "If this continues you have to stop."

I agreed with him. "Let's take it a day at a time."

I walked out of the house, closed the front door, and walked toward the park by our house. When I was walking, I began to feel a deep depressive episode. I thought about how the world would have been better without me in it. *What am I here for on this earth? Why am I continuing to experience depression and sadness every day? Do I want this to be over forever?*

My mind set up a terrible plan that day.

There is a ravine by my home you can walk via a sidewalk with a huge cement railing. If you look down, it goes so far that if a person were to jump over it, they will die. This was my plan on this day. I stood on top of the ravine, and I looked down in despair. My mind was filled with troubling thoughts and tears streamed down my face. I knew this was a side effect from the Lexapro, but they still felt so powerful.

What about the girls and my Tyler? How are they going to deal with the suicide of their mother and wife? How will he take care of them and raise them to know how to be strong women? How am I going to miss gradua-tions, anniversaries weddings, high school graduations, college graduation? What about my family? My mother and sisters, how will they handle me taking my own life? Do I really want to die?

All the sudden I jumped back from the ledge and took a deep breath. I was in complete shock that I almost took my own life. I was in greater shock that I didn't. I promised myself that day that I would never take my own life. It is not fair to myself or my family. My children need a mother. My husband needs his wife.

"The world is better with me in it, "I said to myself. I could not stop crying.

I had to gather myself before I got home, for my girls and Tyler. I could not let them know I was in distress. I wiped away my tears, took deep breaths, and sat on the grass by the ravine for twenty minutes until I was calm. I walked back into the house. I immediately called the doctor.

"Doctor, I need to get off the medications that I am on. I think that my body is having bad reactions to the mixture of all of the medications that you have been giving me."

He sounded angry and annoyed at my request. "Drew, I don't think that it is a good idea for us to work together any longer. The medications that I prescribed are trying to help your symptoms. I just don't think that I can help you any longer."

"That sounds fine. I just think that all of these medications one after the other has done nothing but make me very sick."

"Sorry you feel that way. I just can't help you."

We hung up and I felt so defeated. I just wished the medications had helped me.

He sent me a letter in the mail advising me to "ween" off all the medications, so I did not become ill, which I had been saying to him when he was getting so defensive. All the money Tyler and I had spent was all for nothing.

What I did learn throughout this process is how strong and resilient I am. The strength that helped me choose to live stemmed from knowing that I have so much to live for. I realized how grateful I was that I would be able to see my girls grow up, to not miss any of the milestone moments in their lives. Even though I was thinking of taking my life, I knew that was not an option deep inside of myself. Life is given but once and I had so much more to live.

CHAPTER 10

LETTING GO

I had a choice. Did I keep my father in my life or Did I let him go? I had grappled with this question all these years. I continued to go back. I felt that I deserved how he treated me each time. Everything at first would be great. He would be kind, engaging, easy to be around. Then I would do something to trigger him, and he would become verbally abusive, irritable, and mean. This pattern never changed. Now it was up to me to stop the cycle.

When I had my first daughter Madison, I brought her to meet my father at his office. I had decided after all this time to try to have a relationship with him so he could meet his granddaughter. He looked at her with love in his eyes. I was hoping he would look at me like that. This was one of many times I had hoped my father would feel love for me as his daughter, that me having a child would bring him to be the father to me I always wanted and needed from him. I was always sorely disappointed, expecting something from him that he could not give me. Too much time had passed with many on and offs in our relationship.

I would choose to come in and out of my father's life often. He would get mean and say things that were hurtful, and I would retreat and not want to see him anymore. It was a vicious cycle. I would continue to go back to him wanting some sort of relationship. What I really wanted was my dad to be a "normal" dad, but he just did not have the capability to do so.

I was thirty-eight years old at the time and my girls were five and eight years old. I started to spend time with him, his new wife Betsy, and his stepdaughter Sasha. I wanted to try to develop a better relationship with him and for him to get to know his granddaughters. I was at their home one day, and I found myself looking at pictures of him and Betsy who was not that much younger than he was. I thought how weird it was to see. My parents had been together for thirty years before they decided to get a divorce. That is a very long time that they were together, and for me to see him married to someone else felt strange.

He treated Betsy's children as he had treated his own children—with meanness. When they grew up, they both decided to move far away from Betsy and my father. The difference with his new wife Betsy and my mother was that Betsy was weak with my father, like a door mat. He would verbally abuse her in front of me, I could tell she felt inferior to him. When he would say something mean to Betsy, she would cower and look away, not saying anything. My mother had a mouth and could hold her own with him. When my dad would speak to my mother in a rude way when we were growing up, she always had a quick-witted comeback that shut him up.

My parents fought hard and loved hard. They met in a park when they were in their twenties.

Flirting with her, my dad asked my mom, "Is anyone sitting here?"

She replied, "No." According to my mother he then sat down.

They spent time with one another talking and then they went to eat lunch. After that they were dating and married not long after.

I picked up the picture frame with him and Betsy with my father's arm around her, and it felt strange. I thought, *how can someone be married for thirty years to my mom and then now have a new life with someone else?*

I knew people moved on after divorce. I just always felt even though my parents had a tumultuous marriage, my father always loved my mom. Sometimes when he would talk about her, I could just tell by his tone in his voice and body language that he still felt something for her. He would get vulnerable when he was caught off guard talking about a good memory, he'd had with her. There was love in my parents' marriage even though they had their differences.

My father grew up poor. When talking about his father, my father has said, "He was a nice man who would beat me when I was in trouble." My father did not tell me much more about his father. I do know that he died in a hotel room in his late forties. He had just come back from the war in Korea and gone on a business trip when he died so suddenly. That is really all I know about my father's father.

His mother Janet was mean, and I have not liked her since I was born. My father's stories of his mother were always hateful, saying how mean she was to my father and his younger sibling growing up. He would tell me how she was verbally mean to him a lot, saying things that were very hurtful to him.

Janet would come to our house when we were growing up for visits or Thanksgiving. She would be at the front door for us to greet her and she would bend down and always kiss our dog before us. I always found this odd because my other grandma, my mother's mother, always kissed us first; she never even would acknowledge our dog. Janet was an animal lover and had cats at her house. She seemed to like animals better than people, as she treated animals with more emotional kindness than when she interacted with my father, mother, or us kids.

I could always tell that my father hated his mother just by his nonverbal communication; he was always guarded and seemed anxious when she was around. He would be verbally mean to her and emotionally cold, and you could just tell there was so much more to their story. My father never really wanted to talk about what went on in his house growing up.

I just knew that as I grew older it was now time to break the cycle of abuse with my father. This whole time I kept going back to him to try and have a relationship for him to love, validate, and to be proud of me. The truth was, I never was going to get any of the above. The continued back and forth in the relationship with me waiting for the ball to drop was taking a toll on my mental health. I was always waiting to say or do something that upset him. I was constantly walking on eggshells. After speaking to my father, I would become impatient and irritable with Tyler and the girls. Talking with him gave me such anxiety and I was constantly in fight or flight mode with him. It was not healthy for me.

I decided when I turned forty it was time to let go of my father. I decided one summer day that I wanted to go to my father's office and that would be our last conversation I would ever have with him. This was my way of "letting go." I finally realized that I no longer needed his love and validation for me to be okay within myself. I was chasing a ghost so to speak. He could never be the dad I always needed him to be. It was a cycle I kept going back to that I no longer needed in my life.

It was hot outside in Chicago in the mid-nineties, and I drove to where his office was downtown. I have always had the worst sense of direction, and the neighborhood his office was in it was seedy to say the least. I hoped after the conversation, I would be able to leave and find my car again. I have a horrible habit of parking somewhere and not remembering where I parked. This would not be a good time to lose my car for a couple of reasons. One, after this "letting go" conversation I would be out of sorts, and two the neighborhood was not safe, and I did not want to be robbed or worse.

I had not seen or talked to my father in quite some time before this meeting. I was not sure how he would react when he saw me. I walked into the office and asked the secretary,

"Hi, I wanted to know if my father was available?" She told me to sit down and wait. I was sitting for about five minutes when he walked in.

When he saw me, he said, "Oh, it's you." He smirked. "Come back to my office. We can talk."

I was composed on the outside when on the inside I was overcome with anxiety. I was nervous, and my heart rate was accelerated. We went back to his office and on his office wall right across from his desk was a painting I had made in grade school.

I thought, *how weird he would have my painting and not any from my sisters.*

I refocused my attention on my father who now had a full head of white hair and lines in his face from age. I couldn't help but notice that his eyes looked just like my eyes. It was so strange looking at this man who was my father, seeing features that were just like mine. I had his eyes, his hands, and his legs. I have always had great legs. It's the only good thing that man gave me.

"What are you doing here? Do you want more money for your mother?"

He was always so pissed he had to give my mother money, which is such bullshit because he literally took everything from her when they got divorced. That always made my blood boil when he said that.

"No, actually I am here to talk to you about me."

He looked puzzled and then stood up. "Let's walk."

I thought, *Shit! I am going to not remember where I parked my car!*

"Ok, let's walk."

It was blazing hot out, and he walked so fast. He might not want to be open and talk with me, but I reminded myself that I came here with one purpose—to let him go.

"Dad, I am wanting to tell you that you have daughters, many grandchildren, and you have zero relationships." I went on to tell him about how I felt that I no longer needed his validation in my life to make me feel settled. I gave a long speech of how he was turning seventy and life was too short.

I could feel my face flush and my mouth began to feel dry. I was having so much anxiety wondering what his response would be to my words. My hands were so sweaty, and I was getting short of breath. I tried to compose myself hoping he would not notice I was falling apart inside.

He replied, "I have tried with all of you girls, and it just always ends poorly. I try and it is never good enough for any of you."

I was trying to think of a response that would get through to him to make him understand what I was saying to him.

"Dad, can't you understand that you always seem to get upset with all of us when we don't agree with something you say or do?"

He always had a look on his face like he was elsewhere when he was not paying attention to the conversation, when he was distracted in his own mind. I have always been able to pick up on these times when he was half listening. Nothing from what I said seemed to be registering to him.

"I can't win, Drew. I don't know what you girls want from me."

I realized in this moment nothing I was going to say was going to make my father see what we all needed a father who was present in our lives emotionally. It was becoming a lost cause after all these years.

My father could take no accountability for any of his actions or meanness that he spewed to his children. I was not going to get him to see the reality of the situation. So, I looked at him and said, "I no longer want or need you in my life. You don't bring me peace or happiness."

His response was surprising. "Does this mean you want a relationship?"

I looked at him puzzled and said, "Goodbye, Dad. Take care."

I then walked away feeling proud and vindicated of how I had handled myself.

For the next hour I could not find my damn car. I laughed at myself because I knew this would happen. Since that day, I have had no contact with my father. My life has been better without him in it. I do not feel the ongoing anxiety of when he was in my life. I made the right choice that day to let him go.

CHAPTER 11

PURPOSE

———

I had been a stay-at-home mother for fifteen years, and I wanted to find an independent new purpose in my life. Every day I would wake up to make sure the kids had everything they needed for school—backpacks, lunches, homework that they had finished the night before. Then I would kiss them both goodbye and start my day doing housework, laundry, making the beds, cleaning up the girl's rooms as well as Tyler's and my room. I would take a shower and run errands before the kids came home from school.

I would go to Walgreens to pick up any prescriptions, go to Target to get things that we needed for the house. Then off I would go to the grocery store to get some fruit, yogurt, and other snacks for the kids. When it was 3 p.m., the girls would come home from school, and I would help them get snacks and ask how their days were. If they needed help with homework, I would help with that too. Madison, Sara, and I would figure out what everyone wanted for dinner that evening. I would call Tyler to see how his day was going, if he needed anything from the store, and what he wanted to eat for dinner. I would drive the girls to activities they were involved in for that week. During the weekends I was driving or picking up the girls from friends' houses. Every day of the week was pretty much the same.

I loved being a stay-at-home mom. I just felt that I needed something more for myself as a person. I didn't have a plan for where to apply to use my skills until I started getting curious about a local man I kept seeing around. Every day while I was going to run my daily errands I would drive into town and see a man on a bench. He would be there at 9 a.m. until 6 p.m. every day—rain or shine. I wondered what he was doing there every day and whether he had been dealing with any mental health issues, because he was always talking to himself. I wondered if any facilities in my area helped people. I wanted to get back into working in social services, so I went home and googled mental health facility in the suburb I lived in.

Then it popped up—a residential facility that housed over one hundred people. The website described a place for families to bring their loved ones who had mental health issues. The facility had around-the-clock-care with certified nursing assistants, registered nurses, intake coordinator, fully staffed kitchen, mental health professionals, activities staff, psychologists and psychiatrists. This was a top-notch facility with great reviews from not only residents but families as well. I was impressed by what they had to offer to people who suffered from severe mental illness. It also sounded safe, and I really liked how it catered to the people who lived there. This sounded like a place I would like to work. Everything I was looking for was in this facility.

For some residents, this was permanent housing due to their mental illness being so severe they could not function living independently. For other residents this was a temporary living situation. They needed rehabilitation services, such as: medication distribution, therapy with a psychologist, a psychiatrist to help with medication monitoring, and working with a mental health professional to help set goals. Residents also participated in group therapy and leisure and recreational services. The residents would work on discharge planning with the mental health professionals with some residents going on to live independently and others going to various group homes. It all was dependent on the individual resident and what their specific needs were.

I decided to put together my résumé that week and go to the facility in person to see if they were hiring. A résumé on a computer screen doesn't always capture the real person applying, and I wanted to make an impression, so they could put a face to a name. I wanted them to see I was capable and had a great personality with a work background to match. I had not looked at my résumé in the last fifteen years. I decided I would change the address and make it look cleaner and more updated but honestly, I did not do too much to my résumé. I thought it was already a very good representation of my work I had done prior. I made a copy and put it in a nice folder for when I went to apply for the job.

It was June 2019, and I was wearing a white tank top with forest green cargo pants and sneakers. I dressed casually because I wanted to be approachable and comfortable when I went there. I did not want to seem too eager and overdressed to meet people if they were willing to speak with me.

When I walked into the facility, a young girl was sitting in a chair. I asked her, "Is there anyone I could speak to about a possible job opening?"

I did not know at the time, but one of the mental health professionals had just been let go. The girl told me to wait.

About two minutes later a young woman walked up to me and said, "Hi, my name is Beth. What are you interested in doing?"

With a smile I handed her my résumé and described my social work background. She asked if I would like to take a tour of the facility, which was a pleasant surprise. "That sounds great. I would love to see the building."

The building had four floors, two nursing stations, a library full of books, a table for the residents to read, play cards, and board games if they wanted on the second floor. The library was also used for residents to meet with mental health professionals from time to time.

Mental health professional offices were located on each floor, and I met each one that day. The first worker Beth introduced me to was in her mid-sixties. The second worker I met was a man who was shy and reserved.

Beth then brought me to the second floor where I met another worker named Jenny. She was in her late twenties. When I met her, I had a bad feeling that she was not a good person. I immediately knew in my gut I would not like her. This was my soon-to-be office mate, and she would really give me a run for my money.

I then met the Director of Nursing, Nicole, who was so welcoming. "It was so nice to meet you. I hope to see you again."

I smiled and said, "It was nice to meet you too."

I then met Stacy, the admissions coordinator, who had an abrasive attitude.

Beth then showed me some of the rooms that the residents lived in. There were private rooms and shared rooms. The bathrooms in the private rooms each had a bath with a shower head, toilet, mirror, and a sink. Residents who stayed in private rooms and were not covered by insurance paid three thousand a month.

Shared rooms had two beds divided by a hospital curtain with see-through mesh on top and the solid fabric on the bottom. The bathrooms in these rooms only had a toilet and sink, and they were shared with the room next door. There was a shower room on each floor that the residents could use whenever they wanted. I thought how there was privacy for the residents, which I liked because they treated them as respected individuals.

"A lot of residents have anxiety around taking showers," Beth explained to me. Their solution was set times for residents to shower during the week, some with the assistance of a CNA (certified nursing assistant). Others had no issues at all with showers and would shower daily.

I was happily surprised at how well they took care of the people who lived in the facility, and this made me feel comfortable if they offered me the job. I had worked in a mental health facility as my first job out of college. That facility was dirty, and they did not take care of the building. It had smelled like cigarettes. The building and rooms had been dirty. The staff at the first facility I worked at were sterner with the residents who lived there.

This seemed like a more professional and relaxed atmosphere. This facility took more care in the building and how they treated the residents.

The facility felt a lot like a hospital with nursing stations on each floor, where medications were handed out at specific times for residents. They also had a sun porch where group therapy was held, and some meals were as well. At times when there were no meals, groups, or activities residents could relax at the six tables on the sun porch. TV lounges had couches for the residents to sit on. These were on the main floor and the second floor. Residents would enjoy the shows they agreed to watch together. The cafeteria was in the basement and had vending machines, long tables and round tables that the residents would sit at for scheduled mealtimes. The cafeteria was also used for activities and staff lunch. Beth then brought me back down through a stairwell to a conference room on the first floor. This is where the care plan meetings and staff meetings in the mornings were held.

The residents were all very welcoming and curious to know who I was. Some waved at me, some residents came up to me and asked who I was, and some residents introduced themselves to me. Beth brought me to a resident's room back on the second floor. Beth knocked on the door and said, "Staff."

A man opened the door; he was short, in his sixties, skinny, with a sweatshirt that was as big as him.

He looked at me and said, "Hi, do you want to see my cats?"

At the time, I was confused because I was told there were no pets allowed in the facility. I looked on his perfectly made bed and saw three huge stuffed lions on his bed. His cat slippers were perfectly lined up underneath his bed as well.

"How cool. Thank you for letting me see your cats, and your room is fantastic." He was so proud of how tidy his space had been and was grateful I took the time to speak with him and see his space.

The last person Beth brought me to meet on my tour was the Director of Financial Services, Joanne. From the get-go I could tell that she did not care for me. I was very good at picking up on people's social cues and I could always tell when someone did not like me. When I spoke to her, she was dismissive and not very nice.

I said, "It is nice to meet you."

"Yeah, you too," she replied without any emotion.

I walked upstairs with Beth to conclude the tour. I thanked her and expressed I was really interested in the position, and I looked forward to hearing from her soon.

When I left, I felt so proud of myself. I had not been on an interview in years, and I was prepared when I met Beth. I asked the right questions when it came to the position I wanted. I was calm and poised when I met the staff and the residents. I felt the interview went well. I walked to my car and was excited. I felt I might be offered the job I wanted.

A week later I received a call from Beth asking if I could come in for an official interview, and I went in for the interview the next week.

When I came into the building, Beth asked if I could come into an office so we could talk. I sat down and Beth was sitting across from me at a desk and next to me was Tracy, the assistant administrator. Beth asked, "What do you see yourself doing if you work here? What could you bring to the facility with the skills you have?"

"I really think I could be a great asset to the facility I have worked as a case worker before. I am a fast learner and am very diligent with paperwork."

Beth then asked, "What would you do if a resident was suicidal or wanted to self-harm?"

"I would sit and speak to the resident and document what he or she was saying. I then would get my supervisor for further assistance how to deal with the situation. I would not leave the resident alone due to him or her feeling suicidal or wanting to hurt themselves."

Beth seemed pleased with my answers. I was always good at reading nonverbal communication. She smiled a lot and when I answered a question, she looked at Tracy as if she was happy with my responses. They asked many other questions and I answered all of them articulately and diligently to make sure they knew I was competent to do this job.

It went well. I had brought a list of questions that I wanted to ask. I also had a set salary that I wanted as well. I left the interview feeling confident and proud of myself for being composed, articulate, and prepared. I sent a thank you email to Beth after I got home.

Two weeks later, I received a call. I was in the car with my Madison and Sara when I was offered the position of Mental Health Professional, to start in late September 2019. I was so excited and ready for this new chapter. For fifteen years, I cleaned my house every week, did laundry, ran errands, took care of the girls, picked up and dropped them off at school. I was about to embark on this newfound purpose, to be a working mother and making my own independent money, and I was so ready for it.

CHAPTER 12

MEETING

—

It was my first day at my new job. I wore a tight black tank top, high-waisted camouflage wide leg pants, and sneakers. My makeup was natural and understated, my curly hair was perfectly blown out. I wanted to look professional and put together for the first day. I woke up two hours early because I was excited to start my new job. I felt nervous and was wondering how the staff would be and what the residents were like. Tyler was excited and supportive of me going back to work, he was happy that I had somewhere to be that made me feel happy about helping others.

Madison and Sara were also excited. They said, "Mom, it is so cool that you have a job now. We are happy for you."

They both were independent at getting to school in the morning. Madison would walk to school because we lived so close. Sara took the bus and never had a problem waking up on time and getting to school.

The girls both were set in their routines for the school week. That also put my mind at ease that I would not have to worry about them during the day. It also was comforting to know that if one of them got sick I could easily leave work and pick them up since I was so close to the schools they went to. When they got home from school, Madison had a key to let herself in and then Sara would come home after. They would be doing their homework while I was still at work, and I would come home two hours later. It was a perfect setup for everyone.

I got into my car ready to start my new job and drove there. I entered the building at 8:30 a.m. ready to start the day, even though my hours were 9 a.m. to 5 p.m. I have always been early no matter what time an appointment is, or what time work was starting.

When I walked in, I was met by Tracy, the Assistant Administrator. She told me that she was going to take my picture for my badge that said my name and my position in the facility, and I would need to wear it every day. I put my stuff down in her office and walked with her to the hallway where I stood to have my picture taken. I have always hated getting my picture taken. I will never forget when a woman once said to me, "Oh my Gosh! You don't look like yourself in pictures. You look so bad in this picture! You are pretty. This picture is not." That comment has always stuck with me.

After Tracy took my picture, she handed it to me on a long shoelace necklace that I had to wear. In the picture, I had wrinkles under my eyes that I did not know existed. I was middle-aged but I looked older than I was. The picture could have been worse, but it was not my best.

Tracy took me through the stairwell to the second floor to my new office. When we got there Tracy said, "Drew, this will be your desk, and this is Jenny your office mate." Jenny looked me up and down and fake smiled. I smiled back.

My supervisor, Beth, the woman who had interviewed me, came into our office and was so welcoming. She gave me all the information I needed to do my job. "This is your desk. We have everything set up for you and here is a laptop for you to do your work on."

My office mate Jenny was less than thrilled I was going to be sharing her office, which she shared with me after Beth left the office. "No offense, but I was hoping you were a guy."

"Sorry to disappoint you," I said and laughed at such a rude comment.

"The last woman who worked here was so old; she did not understand how to use any technology, so you are only allowed to ask me two questions. That is it."

I was so taken aback by how rude this young woman was. I had an important realization that first day. Jenny's behavior toward me indicated to me that she felt threatened by how I had a way with connecting to people. Jenny did not have that. She was meek and quiet. The residents did not come to talk to her often whereas from the first day I was there the residents felt immediately comfortable with me and came to speak to me about any issues or concerns they were having. They walked by the office but did not engage much with her at all. I felt in my gut that day she was going to do everything to make me hated in this work environment.

I told myself that first day that I was there to do a job, not to be friends with my office mate. Beth came back that afternoon and wanted to introduce me to the residents on my caseload. She gave me a list of people I would have and then we went door to door to meet everyone. Beth knocked on one of the resident's doors and said, "Staff."

A young man opened the door. He was in his thirties; his head was down but I could see that his skin was pale with dark circles under his eyes.

"Max, this is your new case worker," Beth told him. He timidly looked up at me, and I smiled and introduced myself.

"Hi. I'm Drew. It is so nice to meet you; if you ever want to get out of the building and take a walk, come to my office and let me know."

"Ok, maybe," he said quietly. Then he shut the door.

As we were walking away, Beth let me know that Max had not left the building in almost six months. She expressed to me that he was scared to leave the building due to paranoia and fear. I was fascinated with Max for a couple of reasons. He had kind eyes, and I could tell someone was in there. It felt like the movie *Awakenings* with Robin Williams. He was like Robert De Niro in the movie. He was staring into space and disassociating, but Robin could see life behind those eyes. I thought if I put in the time and effort with

Max, he might not be afraid anymore, and maybe I could help him "awaken."

When I read Max's file, I was blown away at how brilliant he was. He came from a good family who loved and supported him. He was a gifted young man, with so much potential and untapped talent. I thought, *He has the rest of his life ahead of him.* I was determined to wake him up mentally, to have him see hope again in his life.

I continued meeting all the wonderful residents on my caseload that day. They ranged in age from young twenties to mid-seventies. One of the residents I met was named Lyla; she had Schizophrenia and talked to herself but was overall very quiet and shy.

I said to her, "Lyla, my name is Drew. I am going to be your new case worker. Is there anything you would like to work on together?"

Lyla said, "You know what? I have a hard time getting motivated to shower. How about we work on that together?"

I told her I thought that was a great idea. Lyla expressed to me that she had help from a certified nursing assistant during the week. I told her I would check in with the nursing assistant and we would also make this a goal in her care plan. Lyla agreed, and it was the beginning of good rapport between Lyla and me, which was helpful in getting her to trust me to help her.

I met with a man named Kyle. He was in his later thirties and had Schizophrenia. He spent a lot of time in his room and had minimal social contact with others. I spoke with Kyle about his care plan goals. I thought it would be helpful for us to play the game UNO. This way Kyle would be in reality-based conversation, and I could get to know him better.

Kyle agreed that playing UNO sounded fun and he would be happy to play one time a week. I also recommended that he start taking community walks to get some fresh air and have conversations with other residents. Kyle thought that was a great idea and agreed to walking with the other residents in the facility.

With residents who had severe Schizophrenia, constantly hearing voices, hallucinating and delusions, the case worker's job was to have reality-based conversations to ease the intensity of symptoms. I would check on the individuals on my caseload with these symptoms throughout the day to make sure they felt safe and comfortable. Medication could only help them so much since it did not take away the voices, but it did help with agitation and anxiety.

Managing their emotions and making sure they were on the right medications was key to the recovery process for everyone in the facility. It was difficult for so many residents to manage their symptoms from their illnesses. It was a constant effort to continue to have the support of their family. Their treatment team in the facility, the therapists and psychiatrists were so crucial in helping residents try and move toward recovery. Some residents would never fully recover because their symptoms were too severe and their illnesses too debilitating. They were given medication and therapy to help as much as possible with managing their symptoms and their case worker and doctors worked to make them comfortable and feel safe daily.

I was trying to get to know each person individually so I could find the right treatment plan for them to be in a better place with their symptoms. If I could figure out what each resident on my caseload had an interest in, I could get to know them on a personal level to help with their symptoms. I felt so great that I was thinking outside of the box for the residents on my caseload, such as Kyle. When a resident did not feel stigmatized by their illness, and they were treated as a person, it was easier for the resident to manage their symptoms and work with the case worker. They felt supported and this was helpful in their daily recovery.

When I got to work every day, I would always do morning rounds and knock on everyone's door on my caseload. I would say, "Staff," and check that they took their morning medications. I also would make sure that everyone was doing okay mentally. I would go back to my office and do paperwork and then I would have a morning meeting. The rest of the day I would have care plan meetings, meetings with my supervisor, meetings with residents, and I would have my groups that I ran during the day at the facility. Every day was packed with constant work and meetings and the time always passed very quickly.

I worked with more than forty residents, and each one of them was so interesting to work with. I always learned something new when I met with residents. What I loved about this job was that every day was so different from the last and I was always helping people.

It was the end of November, and it was freezing outside. I was walking back from the morning meeting when I turned the corner and saw that waiting outside of my office was Max. He had a coat on, a black sweater, and jeans.

"Hey, can we take a walk now?" he asked.

I was in shock because I did not really think he would trust me enough to walk outside of the building with him.

"Yes, let me put my stuff in my office and get my coat."

I opened the office door with my key, and I put my computer, notebook, pen, and folder on my desk.

I put on my long winter jacket, a hat, and brought gloves just in case. I called down to Beth's office and asked before the walk to make sure it was professional. Beth thought it was an amazing idea and was shocked as well that Max wanted to go outside of the building. Max and I walked out the front door. I looked at him and I could tell he was apprehensive about being outside. He looked around and seemed unsure of his surroundings when we got outside.

I started to have a conversation with Max to make him feel more at ease with his surroundings. I asked Max where he went to college, and he talked about going to NYU. Max talked about music from the nineties, and I told him about how I grew up in the nineties. Max said how fall reminded him of NYU in autumn and how he had great memories from those days. I asked Max how he felt being outside and why he had not left the building before. Max expressed to me that he feared for his life, that people were watching him, and he was being monitored. I reassured him that he was safe, and the walk was almost over. I praised him for trusting me to go with him.

Max and I walked back to the building, and he opened the door for me. He smiled at me and thanked me very politely. I thanked him for trusting me to go on the walk and told him we would have a set meeting time in the morning at 10:30 a.m. Max agreed and walked away. Max had a kindness about him, charm, a quick wit, and a fantastic sense of humor. I could tell this was going to be a case I would feel passionate about.

Seeing Max being willing to try going outside was great, and the day got even better as I was doing rounds. I walked past a resident named Ardy who looked familiar to me. Then I realized I had known Ardy from my first job when I was twenty-two years old working at the first mental health facility.

"Hi, Ardy. My name is Drew. Did you live at the mental health facility in Evanston?"

He smiled. "Yes. I did actually."

"Ardy, I remember you from when I was working there. I was your case worker."

He looked at me in disbelief and said, "I can't believe it. I remember you from so long ago."

I was emotional because he knew me when I was twenty-two and now, I was forty-three years old. He looked the same just with more age on his face. He was a kind man then and he still was such a kind man now. Before he walked away, he said, "Drew, it is so nice to see you again and I am so happy you work here."

"I am so happy to see you too and thank you. I am excited to be working here."

I felt at that moment how strange life can be at times. When I knew him in my twenties, I was so lost emotionally. Now I was a wife and mother. I was so much older, and I felt proud of how far I had come. I was truly grateful to see him again.

I knew I was going to make a difference in the people's lives who I worked with every day, and I did. I helped a lot of people open, go on walks, better manage their symptoms, and make friends in the facility. The people who were on my caseload and even the people who were not felt connected to me. It was not easy for the residents to manage their symptoms on their own. Some residents who were not on my caseload would stop by my office to discuss issues they wanted to talk about that day. I would take the time to be there for them as well.

They knew they had a case worker they could depend on to help them the days I worked, and it felt great that I was able to do so.

CHAPTER 13

UNDERBELLY

There was a sort of normalcy if you came to visit the facility in the daytime. A visitor or family member of a resident who was coming in for just an hour or so would see residents relaxing, playing games, or participating in group therapy. If everyone who was out and about outside of their rooms were managing their symptoms well that day, everything might seem "normal."

What people did not realize was what the people who lived there had to deal with daily mentally. You had to really look beneath the surface of what was going on in the building. I called it "the underbelly." Some residents had Schizophrenia and heard voices all day every day. It was as if someone was whispering in their ear all day long, and there was no way to stop it. This was very difficult for them.

Other residents suffered from obsessive-compulsive disorder from the moment the sun came up until the sun went down. They would repeat rituals such as pacing the hallways, picking up books from the library, putting the books back a certain number of times, and talking to themselves constantly.

Other residents suffered from clinical depression and could not bear to get out of bed all day or shower and take care of themselves. They chose to stay in their room in the dark alone sleeping so they did not have to face how they felt.

The residents who lived there were all there for a reason. Each had a diagnosed mental illness and accompanying symptoms they were trying to learn to manage daily. Some residents were in recovery and the end goal they were working toward was discharge from the facility. The other half of the residents were going to live there forever and never discharge. These residents had severe mental illness and could not function in another type of independent living situation.

Some of the experiences I had with residents still haunt me to this day. The times when I did assessments with residents sometimes exposed me to some very unsettling facts about them.

Every mental health worker had to do assessments for the residents on their caseload. The initial assessment was done when a resident came to live in the facility. During the initial assessment the case worker asked questions regarding the resident's history, where they lived before, how they came to live at the facility, and if any mental health treatment had been given to that individual before coming to live in the facility. A three-month assessment was done for the care plan meeting to assess the goals needed for that resident. This assessment generally continued to occur every three months. Then the yearly assessment reassessed how the resident had been working on their goals that were set for the year at the facility.

During these assessments you really got to know about the mental illness that the individual was dealing with. The case worker asked questions about the thoughts and emotions that individual was experiencing and had had in the past. We also asked questions about whether they had ever experienced any abuse, neglect, suicidal attempts or ideation, self-harm, homicidal thoughts, and many other questions about past hospitalizations and mental health care.

The yearly assessments and the initial assessments were the most emotionally invasive. The questions were about the individual's childhoods, hospitalizations, symptoms, and relationships. These helped the case worker get to know the individual on another level. They also gave the case worker an idea of how severe the illness was on their caseload. The questions on the quarterly assessments were not as intensive as the initial and yearly assessments. They were more focused on how the resident was actively participating in the facility.

I had a new admission in his early twenties, and I had to give him the initial assessment. He had no expression and made me feel very uncomfortable immediately when I met him. When I spoke with him, he looked right through me not at me. I felt an uneasiness around this young man. His actions did not make me feel this way, rather his nonverbal communication made me question what was in his mind. My body felt as if I was in fight or flight mode.

I began to ask him questions, "Have you ever thought of hurting yourself or others?"

His response, "I often think of taking women and holding them against their will."

I was immediately taken aback but could not be reactive. "Can you explain? Do you want to kidnap these women?"

"Well, I liked this girl in grade school, but she did not like me back. Recently, I went to her house and left her a note on her car. I wanted to take her and make her mine."

As I was typing into the computer what he was reporting to me, my body tensed, and my arms and legs pulled closer to my body as if I was protecting myself. I moved my chair farther away from him, so slowly I hoped he would not notice. Me moving mere inches from him made me feel safer, not completely safe during this conversation. Being close to him knowing his thoughts and feelings about women made me uneasy.

"You realize you cannot take women and hold them against their will. Women are people, and it has to be a consensual agreement for her to want to be with or go with you." I wanted him to realize that this thought pattern about women was not normal.

He was unfazed and continued to tell me of his obsessions about women. I went on to ask him the other questions in the assessment and had a plan to discuss what he had told me with my supervisor Beth.

When I finished the assessment, I was honestly worried about the young women in the facility. There was a possibility that he could stalk a woman or many women in the building. I reported to Beth everything he had told me in the assessment. I told her I felt he was not a proper placement for this facility. The residents who lived at the facility were all pre-screened to make sure they were not dangerous to others. He obviously had slipped through the cracks. In his initial interview he had not mentioned anything like he was now divulging to me.

Later that day Beth talked to him about what he had reported to me. He denied saying what he said in his assessment. He called his family and told them he wanted to be picked up and moved out of the facility that day. He was very upset and told her he was leaving and then moved out. I felt better about the fact he would not harm anyone in the facility. If he had not moved out, it could have been a dangerous situation for the women in the facility.

The same week I did an initial assessment with another young man named Dylan in his twenties. He had dark brown unruly hair and wore sweatpants with stains on them and a t-shirt that was also covered in stains. He always was unkempt and never wanted to shower.

Despite that, I felt comfortable with Dylan as he had a softness about him and a nonthreatening demeanor. Dylan was on my caseload and every morning when I did rounds, I would knock on Dylan's door and say, "Staff." He was always sleeping and nonresponsive. It would take ten whole minutes with the help of a certified nursing assistant to wake up Dylan.

I never understood his whole story even after reading his file. During this yearly assessment, I asked about his childhood. I asked who he grew up with and he said, "I grew up with my mom and she would sell me when I was a little boy for sex."

I was very surprised Dylan had shared that with me. He was a man of few words—an observer and not much of a conversationalist. My heart broke at the thought of what Dylan experienced as a child, and I felt overwhelmed with despair knowing he had endured that. It made me realize how much he was holding inside emotionally. I wanted him to feel safe and secure in this conversation.

"Does anyone else know this information about your mother?"

Dylan said, "No, I have never told anyone about it because I get upset."

I thought back to all the children I had helped in foster care, children who experienced similar fates at the hands of their parents. The US Department of Health and Human Services reports that "9.2 percent of victimized children were sexually assaulted. One in five girls, and one in twenty boys is a victim of child sexual abuse."[32]

In Dylan's case, he was not only sexually abused but trafficked as well. Studies by David Finkelhor, Director of the Crimes Against Children Research Center, show that:

Self-report studies show that 20 percent of adult females and 5–10 percent of adult males recall a childhood sexual assault or sexual abuse incident. During a one-year period in the US, 16 percent of youth ages fourteen to seventeen had been sexually victimized. Over the course of their lifetime, 28 percent of US youth ages fourteen to seventeen had been sexually victimized. Children are most vulnerable to CSA between the ages of seven and thirteen. According to a 2003 National Institute of Justice report, three out of four adolescents who have been sexually assaulted were victimized by someone they knew well.[33]

I said, "Dylan, I am so grateful that you chose me to share this with. I am so sorry this happened to you when you were young."

"Well, it's okay. I just play video games and sleep to not think about it."

There was a pit in my stomach, but I was determined to keep my composure. "Where did you go when you got older?"

"My grandma, she saved me. My grandma loved me, and I loved her." Dylan did not want to talk any further about his childhood.

Dylan slept late every day until around noon and spent 80 percent of his time playing video games. In the assessment Dylan showed indications of post-traumatic stress disorder and he also had a history of suicide. It now made sense to me that he was living with the trauma that was his childhood. "Children who were sold for sex are associated with a range of mental disorders, substance abuse, and suicide attempts. Research with adults who were trafficked as children have a higher rate for post-traumatic stress disorder, and anxiety disorders."[34]

Dylan wanted to escape the mental torment of his past by sleeping and paying video games. I felt for Dylan because he did not ask for his mother to treat him that way. At the same time, I felt grateful that Dylan now had a place to be where he felt content and no longer in danger or alone.

Ronnie was another memorable man on my caseload. He had such debilitating obsessive-compulsive disorder. "Obsessive-compulsive disorder is characterized by unreasonable thoughts and fears (obsessions) that lead to compulsive behaviors." More than two hundred thousand new cases arise per year.[35]

Every day he sat in a chair with his head down and his long hair covering his face. He would repeat certain ritualistic behaviors. Ronnie would stand up, sit down, rub his hands together, put his head down, mumble something to himself, lift his arms over his head, and repeat this for hours on end until he was exhausted. Some days he would do this until nightfall.

Other days his roommate Tim had to make sure that he ate. The staff would ask Ronnie to go down to the cafeteria to eat but Ronnie refused. He did not want to eat because it would mess up the rhythm of his rituals. So, the staff would leave a sandwich on his bed for when he was hungry. Some days when I did rounds in the morning Ronnie would be hunched in his chair sleeping, unable to make it to the bed the night before. I would knock on his door and say, "Staff." Ronnie would barely look up at me due to being immersed in his ritual.

"Ronnie, do you need anything?" I wanted to make sure Ronnie was alert and aware.

Ronnie would always respond the same way, "I am fine. Thank you."

Then I would ask his roommate if Ronnie had eaten that morning. Tim always made sure he did and so did the certified nursing assistants. Ronnie would eat and walk around the facility with them for exercise.

Ronnie was such a kind man without a mean bone in his body. He always was so polite to staff and other residents in the building. I was filled with anger at the injustice of such a kind man forced to live with such a debilitating case of obsessive-compulsive disorder. I would think, *why did g-d make his brain sick? Why could he not have a good functioning life?* It was like he was held captive by the behaviors he could not ever escape. Ronnie will be living in the facility for the rest of his life.

When I would ask him about discharge, he would always say, "I am going to stay here. I like it here."

What was so remarkable about Ronnie was that he was an artist. I asked him one day if I could see his work and he agreed. He had pencil sketches that were amazing. He could look at a person and draw them to the last detail. I thanked Ronnie for showing me his art and told him how gifted he was. Looking at the art Ronnie made, I felt overjoyed because I knew when Ronnie was drawing it was the one time his mind was taking a break from the rituals that plagued his mind every day.

So many residents were gifted creatively. Their creativity was an expression of themselves beyond the symptoms and the struggles they encountered daily. Many of the residents who lived in the facility used their creative outlets as part of the care plan goals that were set for them.

One resident wrote poems to his doctor and me for his treatment. He was able to utilize his given talent, which made him focus his mind on something other than his paranoia and delusions; it was a "mental vacation" so to speak. Here is a poem that this resident wrote to the doctor and me.

I CAN'T. I CAN'T. CAN WE? ARE WE ALLOWED? MUST WE CONTINUE? TO DEBASE OURSELVES AND OUR THOUGHTS TO TOTE THE PARTY LINE? GOD, FORBID WE STEP OUT OF LINE. HATE THEM, HATE OURSELVES, HATE EVERYONE.

WE ARE THEY, IN A ROCK PIT OF NO BOTTOM WE FREE FALL FROM IT FOR 20 YEARS. BEST NOT TO LOOK, BEST NOT TO CRY, I HOPE NO ONE SEES ME. PLEASE DON'T HATE ME, I'M JUST LIKE YOU. I CARE, I HAVE A FAMILY, YOU DON'T UNDERSTAND AND YOU WON'T. I CANNOT BEAT YOU, STAY AHEAD OF YOU, THERE IS NO WINNING.

I DON'T WANT ANYTHING YOU WANT BUT THE RIGHT TO PURSUIT LIFE, LIBERTY, AND THE PURSUIT OF HAPPINESS. YOU DON'T CARE. RULE NUMBER ONE, YOU'RE WORTHLESS. DO YOU RESPECT THAT. EVEN IN MY MOST COMFORT ZONES I FEEL I CANNOT ADDRESS THE MOST FUNDAMENTAL ISSUES. YOU WILL ALWAYS WIN.

THINGS NEED TO STOP; THINGS NEED TO CHANGE. I AM NOT ALONE.

This resident wrote this poem off the top of his head. It took him just five minutes to write it.

The underbelly of the facility also came out in residents' feelings of depression, thoughts of suicide, self-harm, and anxiety. I met with many residents who were having these dark thoughts.

What the residents did not realize was that I understood exactly how they were feeling. How it felt to have the dark feelings of not wanting to be here anymore. Or thoughts of wanting to hurt myself. Like I would remind myself, I always had to remind the residents I worked with that acting on these thoughts was never an option.

These thoughts are so difficult and painful in the moment, but there is always a light at the end of the feeling. I lived with this mantra in my mind too. I had to use my training and skills to work through with the residents when it was so hard for them to deal with the dark struggles in their minds.

I was walking to my office when I passed a women named Rebecca in the hallway. She was not acting her usual self. Every time she saw me, she would wave hello and smile at me. This day she did not say anything as I passed her and instead, she looked down at the floor. Something was off that day with Rebecca.

"Rebecca, are you okay? What is going on? I noticed you seem sad."

Rebecca looked up at me with tears welling in her eyes.

"Drew, I am having such a hard time today."

"I am sorry. Why don't you come to the library so we can talk?"

Rebecca was so upset she was shaking, crying, and stuttering.

"Rebecca, look at me and take a deep breath, let's process the emotions you are going through."

I wanted to get Rebecca to a calm and peaceful state so she could not induce a panic attack. The calmer I was the calmer Rebecca would become.

"Rebecca, do you feel like hurting yourself?"

She looked at me and I already knew the answer.

"Yes."

"Do you want to kill yourself?"

"No."

I went into my office across from the library table where we'd been sitting. I got a sheet that said, "Self-Harm Agreement." On this sheet of paper, we listed the resident's name, date. It had three lines for three coping skills the resident writes down. Rebecca and I filled out the self-harm agreement and we both signed at the bottom.

"I am going to have to check on you every hour for the next three hours."

"That sounds good. I am calming down."

As we sat together, I could see the dark cloud begin to lift. Rebecca and I both stood up and I asked her, "Can I give you a hug?"

She said, "Yes, of course."

I embraced Rebecca and she hugged me back.

"You are so strong. Don't ever forget the strength you have inside."

Humans have a natural need for human connection and feeling valued, cared for while needing support from others. Rebecca needed human connection in that moment when she felt as if she was alone.

I wanted Rebecca to know she was not alone, and she had the emotional support she needed in that difficult moment for her. I was so grateful that I could be of help in the moment that she needed it most.

I checked on Rebecca an hour later and she was back to her baseline, which was calm and balanced as she had been the day before. The rest of the day, I checked on her and she felt better. Rebecca did not go to the hospital for feeling like she wanted to hurt herself, and instead she used all her skills that we had written down. I was so proud of her for being so strong.

Later that day I found a note on my desk from Rebecca that read:

In a way you can't imagine, you made a difference to me caring in a very scary moment. You don't know how much it mattered. Thank you, Rebecca.

Therefore, I loved coming to this job every day. It felt rewarding to help people who needed support when they could not help themselves. In all my work with the residents, I aimed to give them the human connection they needed, and I believe I was successful at doing this. So many times, when I ran group therapy, I was told by so many residents that the way I worked with the people at the facility was so impactful.

A resident named Sandra said once, "Drew, you have a gift with people and the residents here know how much you care for them."

That statement coming from Sandra made me feel I was helping the people I worked with every day.

Despite the underbelly of pain and trauma at this facility, the work I was doing was making a difference.

CHAPTER 14

COVID

———

It was March 23, 2020, a Monday morning, when I woke up with a temperature of 100.6, headache, body aches, nausea, loss of taste and smell. Covid was just becoming more rampant in the United States. I have asthma and am high risk due to the respiratory complications that can come from having it. There were still so many unknowns about the virus, and this filled me with fear at the possibility of having it.

I called Rush Hospital in Chicago because I knew they were the best with the Covid-19 outbreak. I was watching the news that morning and saw a man who had Covid talking about the care he was receiving and how outstanding the hospital had been taking care of him in this crisis. I also read that Rush was doing a great job with the handling of the pandemic. "Rush set the standard for Covid-19 care and received national recognition for its preparedness. In spring of 2020, Rush was able to successfully care for the sickest of Covid-19 patients, receiving hundreds of transfers from other hospitals that couldn't provide the care that patients needed."[36] I told the nurse on the phone my symptoms and she told me to come in at 6 p.m. for a Covid-19 test.

Tyler and I went to the appointment an hour before the scheduled time because it took an hour to get there. Tyler told me to get in the car and on the way to the hospital I felt very sick. My head was pounding, and I felt feverish and nauseated. My skin was pale and clammy, and I felt weak. When we drove up to the building a man with a face shield, mask, gloves, all the protective gear for the virus met us. He had a walkie talkie and told the nurses on the other end that I was here for a Covid-19 test. I was told to get out of the car and the man escorted me to the doctor's office for the test.

When I walked in everyone was in protective gear to make sure they were not exposed to the virus. It looked like it was out of a sci-fi movie. Face shields, N95 masks, gloves, protective gowns, shoe coverings; I had never seen anything like this before. The nurse first took my temperature, and I did not have a fever at the time. Then she took my oxygen, it was low, and she was very concerned.

I said, "I feel very weak and my body aches."

The nurse said, "Drew, your oxygen is very low, and I need to know your other symptoms."

I told the nurse, "I have had an on-and-off fever of 100.4 to 102.0 on and off throughout the day, stomach pain, loss of appetite, debilitating headaches, joint and muscle pain, I cannot sleep, dry cough on and off, and a sore throat."

The nurse said," Because of your symptoms and low oxygen I am bringing you over to have you further assessed."

The nurse gave me a Covid-19 test and decided it was in my best interest to go to the Covid garage to be given a physical by the doctor there.

I called Tyler and told him I had to be assessed due to my symptoms and condition. Tyler said, "Keep me updated. You will be okay."

The nurse put me in a wheelchair and wheeled me into a huge garage with plastic chairs that sat six feet apart. Tents there looked like a scene out of ET when they brought Elliot to get tested with plastic everywhere; I was terrified. I looked at the nurse with tears streaming down my face. "Please don't leave me here. I am scared."

She looked at me in her protective goggles, which were fogging up because she also had tears. It was very emotional as she put her gloved hand on my shoulder and said, "You will be well taken care of here. I promise you will be okay." Then she walked away back to the hospital.

I was then checked in by other women wearing an N95 mask. I had to stand behind a rope that separated us, so we were six feet apart. She asked me my age, address, and other medical questions and then told me to take a seat and wait. I got up and sat with the ten other masked sick people waiting to get into the tent to see the doctor.

At hour five a young girl in her twenties walked up to the chair next to mine. She literally looked like she was deathly ill. Her skin was flushed as though she had a very high fever, and she looked weak with her eyes bloodshot, and her hair matted down and greasy. I loudly said, "I am sorry. You cannot sit here. There are a lot of empty chairs."

I could tell by her eyes that she was so angry. She said, "Whatever!"

An hour went by, and all the sudden nurses were rushing behind me. I turned around and the young sick woman who was going to sit next to me was passed out cold. The nurses were pounding on her chest to revive her, and she gasped for air as she woke up and was rushed into the ER. This was all getting too real; sitting there not knowing who had the virus and who did not was scary. I was in an enclosed garage with people in masks and I just did not feel safe sitting there for so many hours.

After six hours of waiting to be called for the doctor in the Covid tent, it finally was my turn. The doctor asked me a ton of questions and physically examined me. When he felt my lower back I had sharp pains, He was concerned and wanted me to go to the ER for X-rays.

"I am concerned about your kidneys. It is better to be safe and get an x-ray to check out what is going on."

I said, "Okay. I will wait to get into the ER. Thank you for seeing me. Stay safe."

I called Tyler and told him it would be another four hours before I would be out. I had x-rays taken, blood drawn, and they could not find anything wrong with me, so they sent me home. The doctor told me I had to quarantine when I got home and not be around my kids and Tyler. They were not yet sure if I had the virus. I needed to wait for the results of my Covid test. They told me it would be at least five to ten days to get the results back.

I had to be quarantined for six days and six nights. Tyler had to sleep in another room just in case I had the virus. The days that I was in my room my symptoms were brutal. I felt ill with chills, fever on and off, no appetite, no taste and smell, body aches, the list goes on. I have had the flu before, but I never have felt this sick.

It was so strange not being able to leave one room for all those days. It was very hard not to see Tyler and the girls as I was used to seeing them every day. I felt lonely, and it was hard to take up the space of the time each day. I Face Timed my friends and family to keep them updated, we would have long conversations about how I was feeling and what was going on with them. It was nice when I had these phone calls because it made me feel less alone. I also slept a lot since I was very fatigued. Watching TV took up big chunks of time in my days. When I was hungry Tyler would make me food and bring it to the door with a mask on. I was grateful that he was able to take care of me and the kids when I was sick.

When I got a call from the hospital, they told me the results came back negative. I believed I had the virus. I had all the symptoms and have never felt that sick before. I suspect the timing of my test had something to do with the results coming back negative. "Results may be affected by the timing of the test. For example, if you are tested on the day, you were infected, your test is almost guaranteed to come back negative because there are not yet enough viral particles in your nose or saliva to detect."[37]

The Executive Director at the facility agreed to have me work from home for the next three months since I was considered high risk if I got Covid. I also could run my group therapy from Zoom. I ran four groups each week—Feelings group, which was twice a week, Smoking Cessation group, and Wellness group. It was so important for the residents to come to these groups, especially during the pandemic, because the residents were not allowed to leave the building except for walks with activities. The groups gave them something to look forward to and they could engage with others and not just be isolated in their rooms.

When I worked from home, I was working out of my sunroom, which has a huge round table that faces our lush backyard. It was the perfect setup for my job. I woke up every morning as if it was a regular workday. I would start my day by logging into my work computer and reading the staff log of what was happening in the facility the night before.

All the staff were connected through the computer to keep all staff updated on all the residents in the facility. We would have morning meetings on a group chat, and everyone would take turns discussing their caseloads. The nursing staff would discuss any changes with an individual's behaviors or medications. The meeting usually lasted for an hour and a half.

I would then go through my call list and call each resident who had a phone on my caseload. For the residents who did not own a phone, Beth would make sure they could use the office phones so I could do a check-in with them as well. I would tell the residents that if they needed me to contact me on my cell phone. After speaking with them I would document our conversations.

I worked on the residents' care plans on my caseload. The care plans had set goals for everyone to work on with me for the next three months. If I had assessments to do, I would call or FaceTime residents I needed to speak with.

It was interesting because now I was getting to know the residents on a more personal level. I had a man on my caseload named Lenny who was in his late sixties. He always had disorganized speech when he met with me at the facility. He had more organized speech when we had our FaceTime calls. He was such a lovely person to talk with. When I would FaceTime him, he would say, "Hi, Drew! Am I talking to a movie star!"

He would say this every time I called him, and it always made me laugh. This guy was a professional thrift shopper before the pandemic. He would take the train to the city and find the most unbelievable finds. He would literally find a brand-new Apple computer for fifty dollars. He was a good man and quite a character.

Peter, who was on my caseload, was always avoiding our weekly meetings at the facility. When I talked to him, he would usually give me a brief answer and walk away. When I worked from home it was amazing how open and vulnerable Peter was on the phone. I asked Peter about where he lived before the facility. He went into detail about how he had anger issues and had a lot of depressive episodes that were very hard for him to manage when he lived at home with his parents. The phone seemed to make Peter feel safe talking with me. He was so at ease and open to share stories of his life and his relationships with his family.

From Peter being more open with me, I realized how resilient he was, which was truly remarkable; he had been through so much in his life and had such a positive attitude. Peter and I would speak sometimes twice a week. Each phone call was better than the last, and Peter became more trusting of me. I was so grateful that I had the chance to get to know him on a different level than when I was working in the building.

Some calls made me laugh. Two women on my caseload lived together in the same room. Sandra and Emily were as different as you could imagine. Emily was soft spoken, shy, a book worm. Sandra was eccentric, loud, and always social in the facility. They would call me separately to complain about the other to me.

Emily would say, "Drew, Sandra is taking all of my money and cigarettes. What do I do?"

I would say to Emily, "tell Sandra she has her own money and cigarettes. To please stop taking yours."

Then I would get the call from Sandra an hour later, "Emily, will not leave me alone she talks to me all day. It is making me nuts!"

I would say, "Sandra, just tell Emily nicely to please leave you alone for a while."

Then Sandra loudly would agree and hang up the phone. This calling me and telling on one another happened the whole three months I worked from home. Every time the phone rang, I would laugh to myself; it was like a comedy show.

I also would Face Time Max. During these phone calls I could tell what mental state he had been in. It was amazing that just from seeing his face I could assess whether he was doing well or whether he was having a horrible mental health day with the medications and any other issues, he might have been having that day. He seemed to still be moving toward recovery even though our meetings were remote. I was grateful for this due to the fact we had done so much work for his recovery. I did not want him to regress mentally.

It was remarkable how well working from home during Covid-19 went. I worked from home for three months before I went back in person to the facility. I felt excitement and readiness to go back to the facility to interact in person with the residents. Working from home went very well, but I am a people-person, I was itching to get back to the facility and see people and get back into the building to do my job.

CHAPTER 15

RECKONING

I felt excited to be back working with the people I so enjoyed helping everyday but the fear of going back to work after three months of working from home was very real for Tyler and me. We had to make sure that we had a plan in place to keep me safe, so I would not contract the Covid-19 virus.

At that point there had been more than "forty thousand confirmed cases and 473 deaths in the United States."[38]

A vaccine had not been created yet, so the risk was high for the general population to get the virus. The estimates at the time showed "nine people per thousand US Covid-19 cases would die of the disease."[39]

I told Tyler I was going to make sure to bring sanitizer with me as well as a mask, and I was never going to meet with more than one person at a time. We also decided that after work I would wash my clothes and shower to be extra safe. We had an effective safety plan for me and our family.

The morning I drove to work after being gone for so long my stomach was in knots not knowing if I would be able to avoid the virus at work. I was sweating and felt nervous inside as I tried to get calm before walking into the facility. I had to gain composure of myself. I did not want the other staff or the residents to see I was worried about being in this environment. I had no idea what working in person during a pandemic was going to be like. I did not want to be in fear. I wanted to have a steady mind that also was taking all the precautions to stay safe.

When I got back to work everyone was happy to see me—except Jenny. My first day back, we were in our office, and she said, "Can I tell you something?"

"Sure. Go ahead."

She went on to tell me that since I had worked there, she was making up stories to staff to get me fired.

"Why would you do that to me?" I asked her.

Her response in these exact words was, "It was because I was jealous of the work you were doing; I wanted recognition like you were getting."

I told her I was hurt by her actions behind my back, and I did not know what to say to her. I got up from my chair and walked to my supervisor Beth's office.

"You cannot believe what I am going to tell you. Jenny just told admitted to me she was making up lies about me to staff and residents to get me fired."

I thanked her and she told me that she would see me in the morning meeting.

It was time for the morning meeting with all the case workers, Beth the executive director, Joanne, Tracy the director of nursing and many other staff. At the beginning of the meeting Jenny stood up and said, "I wanted to let everyone know that since Drew has worked here, I have made up lies to all of you about her to get her fired." The room was silent as everyone sat wide-eyed and in shock.

Tears were streaming down my face because of all the poor treatment from the other staff toward me during the time I had worked there. What was it for? Lies, a bunch of lies that I knew nothing about. The staff who were not nice to me would whisper behind my back as I walked by. They would not say hello back when I said hi to them in the morning or throughout the day. In a meeting once, Mel, the case worker, called me stupid in front of all the staff in the meeting. All of this was because of the lies Jenny was spreading to the staff. My character as a person was assassinated due to Jenny's lies.

What was so unbelievable to me was that four of the staff members who Jenny was friends with were comforting her after the fact that she admitted to being a liar. Not one person apologized to me for how they had treated me all this time. The whole situation made me sick to my stomach.

After the meeting I went back to my office. Jenny was there with Beth behind her instructing her to get all her belongings in a box for her to leave.

"Can I ask you a question? What were you saying about me?" I asked Jenny.

"That is not appropriate for you to ask. I am not discussing it with you." Jenny then handed me the key to the doctor's office on our floor that she had. After Jenny packed a box with her belongings, Beth told her she had to leave. Jenny was escorted out of the building by Beth, the admission coordinator, and one other staff member after she was formally fired.

It was finally time for Jenny's reckoning. I have always believed in karma, "the force generated by a person's actions held in Hinduism or Buddhism to perpetrate transmigration and in its ethical consequences to determine the nature of the person's next existence. Destiny or fate, following as effect from cause."[40] To put it simply, when someone treats someone, else unkindly there is always a way the universe pays that person back. I felt this was truly Jenny's payback for her poor treatment of me while I had done nothing to ever make her feel bad or upset in any way.

After Jenny left, I felt like I could finally breathe knowing I was no longer being talked about. I went on with my work in the facility.

That same day I thought of a great idea for Max to move forward with his ongoing recovery. Since Max and I had built a trusting foundation, he was ready to go for regular walks outside to challenge his paranoia and delusions. I told my idea to Beth, and I also asked the executive director if I could continue to go on walks with Max one time a day. This was a way to have reality-based conversations and to challenge his fears of being outside.

I met with Max at our 3:30 p.m. meeting. I told him the idea to further his recovery. He thought it was a great idea and was up for the challenge. I told Max we would walk at 12:45 p.m. every day to get him out of the building.

The next day at 12:45 p.m. Max showed up at my office and we walked outside of the building. Max and I had not taken a walk since my first couple months of me working at the facility. During the walk, Max said, "Do you see that FedEx truck that looks suspicious?"

"That is there because a lot of people are ordering online because of the pandemic."

He nodded and said, "This is helping. Because by you telling me what the trucks are there for, I feel less anxious and predated upon."

I told Max the whole purpose of this exercise every day was to have him challenge his thoughts and hopefully that would make him feel less afraid and paranoid. I told him the more we discussed normal topics, the more normalized he would feel. The walk was a success and Max expressed to me that "It felt good to get out of the building and breathe in the fresh air."

I started to see a drastic change in Max's behaviors and emotions. He was completely in recovery, no longer the meek boy at his parents' care plan meeting. Max now had confidence and felt that he could think about his future discharging from the facility one day. Max and I walked every day for three months up until the day I quit the facility for good.

The last month that I was working, Max would be ready to go for our walks at the front door of the facility. He would be showered with clean clothes on every day. He was mentally getting stronger and less afraid. Max also began to go to Feelings group, which was a big shift for him. Max did not feel comfortable being in large groups of people, but one day he said to me, "I am ready to start integrating into the facility more." I really could see how the walks were making Max more comfortable in his environment outside of his room.

The Feelings group I ran on Thursdays at 3 p.m. usually had seventeen residents and it was held on the sun porch on the second floor. With worries about the virus, everyone had to sit six feet apart and we were only allowed six people in the group. Still, Feelings group remained a wonderful resource for the residents. It was amazing how open and emotionally vulnerable residents would be. They would share their thoughts and feelings regarding the topic discussed and give their own personal examples of how the topic affected them on a personal level.

The first group I ever held at the facility I had chosen the topic of the stigma of mental illness. I wanted to hear from the residents how living with a mental illness affected them directly. I was amazed by the reactions I heard in the group. One resident talked about how the stigma of his mental illness made him feel sad.

He said, "When I sit outside on the porch, people who walk by go to the other side of the street because they are afraid of people who live in the facility."

Unfortunately, this is just one example of how people with mental illness face discrimination. "Discrimination may be obvious or direct, such as someone making negative remarks about your mental illness or your treatment. Or it may be unintentional or subtle, such as someone avoiding you because the person assumes you could be unstable, violent or dangerous due to your mental illness."[41]

He went on to talk about how it made him feel bad about himself and judged by the people in the community. I thanked the man for sharing and expressed to the group that people who do not understand mental illness should try to take the time to get to know what it is about and not pass quick judgment. The whole group talked about how having a mental illness made them feel unloved, vulnerable, and not normal in society. This discussion really hit home for me. I too felt the stigma of mental illness. I felt like I had to hide my illness and was an actress half of the time. I was hiding my symptoms from my friends and people I met so I would not be thought of as lesser than. That way I didn't have to be put in the "not normal" category.

I expressed to the group how everyone who lived in the facility was taking care of themselves mentally through therapy, medication, and they all had a great treatment team. I went on to discuss how women and men not living in the facility sometimes self-medicate to forget about their anxiety, depression, and other mental illnesses they experience with alcohol, drugs, and other substances and engage in unhealthy behaviors to not have to cope with their feelings. "Research shows that mental illnesses are common in the United States, affecting tens of millions of people each year. Estimates suggest that only half of people with mental illness receive treatment.[42]

You could tell something was registering in the group because a resident said, "Drew, I never thought of it that way. We are just normal people dealing with our issues." I agreed and told the group how honored I was to be able to be there to give a different perspective about mental illness. I knew I had to continue to find topics in these groups to give the residents a voice.

I began to really get the hang of touching on the subjects the residents felt passionate about. For the first time, the residents told me they felt like someone wanted to hear them. During one Feelings group, I talked about mental illness and how it affects families. I did this to get input from the residents, but I also learned a lot about how helpful and supportive family can be. One woman from my caseload named Laverne always attended my Feelings group.

Laverne had red, curly, frizzy hair and wore a lot of fabulous makeup. She always was wearing an outfit that was, well, let's say an attention getter. In the summer, she would wear a bright pink sports bra, bright pink spandex shorts, and she always had a huge purse on her arm. This purse would be filled with at least five packs of cigarettes, her wallet hanging out, and papers that she would carry all stuffed inside the bag.

Laverne would talk in group about her family who loved and supported her no matter what. Laverne always spoke highly of her sister who had a lot of money and paid for Laverne to stay at the facility. Her sister would send her clothing, endless amounts of cigarettes, and she always made Laverne feel loved.

A woman on my caseload named Karen would come to my Feelings group sometimes. She was soft spoken and always carried a bag with her belongings in it. She had a fear of people taking her things, so she always carried them with her.

One day Karen had a care plan meeting, and her sister Emily came. Every resident's family was invited to their care plans. Not many of the residents' families showed up for their meetings but Karen's sister Emily never missed a care plan meeting.

When Emily showed up for the meeting, it was as if I was looking at Karen well and not ill. Emily looked identical to Karen. They had the same face and the same color hair and eyes. It was uncanny. Emily was dressed in perfectly fitted jeans with her nails manicured, a very nice sweater, makeup perfectly placed, and her hair was blonde like Karen's but a little shorter and you could tell she had just been to the salon.

This connection between Karen and her sister Emily was one I will never forget. At the meeting the case worker, Director of Recreational Services, Dietetic Service Supervisor, Director of Nursing and the resident were all present. I always started the care plan meeting by discussing the goals for the next three months. I would then get the resident's input about the goals. The meeting continued with each staff person talking about how the resident was doing that quarter.

After all the staff had spoken, I asked Emily if she had anything to add. She looked at all of us with tears in her eyes. She took Karen's hand in hers and said, "I wish I could take all of the voices and darkness out of my sister. I wish I could just have my sister back."

Everyone at that table felt the love Emily felt for Karen. Karen looked back at her Emily and said, "I love you. Thank you for coming."

It took everything in me to not break down crying. After the care plan meeting, I went to the staff bathroom where I sat on the floor and cried. I could not understand the pure and raw love I witnessed. It was so wonderful to see such acceptance from a family member of a woman so ill mentally. Many family members of the residents in the facility did not cope with their illness well at all. They either did not speak to them or did the bare minimum by calling them once a month or sending them money.

"A diagnosis of a mental illness affects the whole family. It might bring strain on relationships that go above and beyond the effects it has on the individual. They usually arise because of the differences in understanding what a mental illness is and how to best deal with it. It can lead to fractures in families, serious disagreements, and sometimes estrangement."[43]

These were the moments in this job for me that made me face my own illness and recovery. Many days I would realize I was being taught by the people who lived there about myself and my mental illness. They never knew how much they all meant to me, but I was so grateful they all came into my life to teach me that I was not only resilient but that I was just like them. The only difference between the residents and me was that I wore a mask every day that looked perfect on the outside. Nice clothing, makeup, manicures, pedicures, wealth, but inside I was in pain. The emotional pain that all the residents I met with talked about was often the same kind of pain I was experiencing.

I was helping them deal with their symptoms and feelings but who was helping me? I often asked myself this when I would leave at the end of the day. By working with people with severe mental illness, I was taking in all their emotions every day. It was one thing to deal with a friend having a bad day. It is quite another to deal with residents who were having severe depression, thoughts of self-harm, anxiety, post-traumatic stress symptoms—on top of having to regulate residents' emotions who were hearing voices and seeing hallucinations during the day.

I always had to have a calm and balanced mind while working with this population of people. I did not have to think about my own mental health issues when my mind was so focused on others' thoughts and emotions.

I was pushing my emotions away to not deal with what I was going through. I was not in therapy or on any medication when I was working at the facility. Not until I quit the job there would I finally get the right medication and therapy I needed.

CHAPTER 16

QUIT

A voice inside of my head one day when I was at work said, "It is time for you to quit. Your family needs you." I was putting so much time and energy into my work at the facility that I was losing my connections with my husband and kids. Before I went back into my career, I had always put them first. Before I worked, I was emotionally available for the kids and Tyler.

Before I worked, Tyler always left early in the morning before the kids went to school. I was usually still sleeping when he left, but I would always feel him kiss me goodbye on the forehead. It was comforting to me that he did that still after all our years together. Doing his best not to make any noise, Tyler would get his coffee and then quietly shut the door, leaving for the day in the city.

Before I got my job at the facility, I would talk to Sara about her day ahead before she got on the bus that morning. Sara being a tween would be nonstop talking. She was excited about everything, and every other word was "literally." We always laughed before she went to school; Sara has a personality that is funny and playful.

I would say to her before she got on the bus every day, "Have a good day. I love you. See you when you get dropped off after school."

Sara would look back at me smiling, backpack on her shoulder. "Love you. See you later."

Madison walked to school every day. She is not a morning person, much like me. I would ask her about what her day would look like, and she would say to me, "It is a lot of classes and a lot of work." Madison did not want to engage in much conversation in the morning. Being fifteen Madison never was thrilled about anything and was often quiet on her phone. I would say as she was walking out the door, "Love you. Have a good day. I will see you when you get home."

Madison always said, "Bye. Love you." As she was walking out the door, she was still looking down at her phone. I would smile to myself as she left because I remembered what it was like to be that age. Nothing much mattered except your social life.

When the kids were at school I would do laundry, make the beds, clean the house, and take out our dog Sam. Each day was filled with household chores and errands until I would be home for Sara when she walked in from school. Madison would get home around 2:30 p.m. from school and would go upstairs to do her homework for the next day.

I would help the kids with any homework they had. I am a horrible cook, so Tyler mostly did the cooking. I would help set the table. After dinner, I would spend time asking the girls about their days, friends, and anything else they wanted to talk about. Madison and Sara usually spent the rest of the evening on social media or talking to their friends on FaceTime on the phone. Before they went to sleep, which was usually around 10 p.m. or later, I would open their doors and say, "Love you. I will see you tomorrow." Then the next day would be like the day before.

Tyler was usually exhausted from his workday in the city. He usually got up at 5 a.m. and would sit in traffic to the city for an hour or more. Then he would be in nonstop meetings all day and on the phone. We would usually talk about our days at the dinner table. Then we would watch some TV and Tyler would go up to bed early and watch more TV. I would stay up late and watch my shows until about 12:30 a.m., and then I would go to bed.

Now that I was working, I was running four therapeutic groups a week, I had forty-plus people on my caseload, and I was working some Saturday nights 7:30 p.m. to 10:30 p.m. I came into work at 8:30 a.m. and stayed until 5 p.m. every day. Some nights, I would even stay later if a resident was having a crisis.

When I got home, I felt emotionally checked out. I would walk in the house and before I would even talk to Tyler and the girls, I would have to shower. I also had to wash my clothes I wore that day due to the safety precautions I was taking with Covid-19. I did not want to put my family at risk because I was working around people all day long. I felt physically and emotionally drained at the end of the day.

All day for eight hours I was helping people and talking non-stop. When I got home, I did not want to talk at all. I just wanted to be alone and relax. I could feel myself being distant as the girls talked about their days. I would see their lips moving but I was barely paying attention. I was also very irritable.

Sara would say, "Mom, can you help me with this math problem?"

I would snap at her and say, "You know I am bad at math. Ask Dad!"

I could see in her face it made her feel bad and I felt guilty for my reaction. I was just so overstimulated from my workday. When I was home, I needed quiet, and I could hardly handle conversations. I felt as if every day I was being pulled in two opposite directions that I could not balance.

I felt so awful about wanting to quit because I had left several times prior when due to the stress of Max being taken off my caseload and Covid. I really felt bad for the residents because mental health workers came and went all the time.

"The rates of turnover in publicly funded mental health settings range from 30–60 percent annually."[44] "Staff burnout predicted increased turnover, staff reported leaving their organizations because of personal, organizational, and financial reasons; just over half of staff that left their organization stayed in the public health sector."[45]

It was hard on the residents to always have new case workers when they gained trust in the one prior. I knew it was going to be difficult for so many residents that I knew and worked with daily. I just knew in my heart that I needed to take care of myself and my family first.

I knew I would end up divorced if I did not put any effort into my marriage or my family. I needed to also be present for my girls. They needed me. "Juggling child-care challenges with work responsibilities takes a toll. There are thirty-five million working mothers in the US at the end of 2019 and roughly 9.8 million working mothers in the US suffering from workplace burnout."[46]

I could not balance being a wife and a mother and working all at the same time. I was experiencing the burnout of having to do all of it every day. I had to choose one or the other, and losing my family was not an option.

I had Beth meet me in my office. I felt nervous and flushed. I was embarrassed that I was quitting again. "Beth, I know this is awful for you to hear but I am going to be leaving this job for good, and my last day is in three days." I felt the sooner I left the sooner I could get back to being there for my kids and Tyler.

Beth said, "Drew, I completely understand your family has to come first." I was so grateful that Beth was so understanding about my situation.

Now I had to prepare myself to tell all the residents. Over the past year, I had grown to care about all the residents in this facility, even the ones not on my caseload. I could tell you at least one thing about each person who lived in that building. I took the time to really listen and get to know every one of them. I let my caseload know I would be leaving. I am always honest, so I told them I had to go back to being a stay-at-home mom. Everyone said they understood why I had to leave. They expressed sadness for my departure, but they also understood.

A resident named Lucy would always stop by my office to tell me about how she was working with The Moving on Program. She would also share her poetry and art sketches with me. This young lady was beyond talented, and she was beautiful inside and out. Lucy gave me a painting she had done one of the last days I was working. The back of the painting read:

Dear Drew, I don't think I've ever met somebody who works as hard as you. You are about everybody shining because that's what you love and that's what you strive for. Wherever you go has super lucked out. The world needs Drews right now. I think you make everybody want to be a better person. Even when people don't want to smile, I feel like they are cared about it's a unique superpower of yours. Not an ending for you, just a new colored beginning. Although I'm sure you knew that. Keep surprising everyone and rocking gauchos—Lucy—

Tears streamed down my face as I read her letter. I thanked Lucy and asked if I could give her a hug. She said, "Yes."

I stood up and I hugged her. I was so grateful to her that she had taken the time to create this beautiful painting. The words that she wrote I keep with me on my phone. I took a picture of her words to remind myself that I am enough and that I made a difference. I put her painting in our library so I can look at it every day and remember all the amazing residents I worked with.

The one person I knew it would be so hard to break the news to about me leaving was Max. He showed up for our regular scheduled walk, and as we walked out of the front of the building I said, "Max, I have to tell you that I decided I am no longer going to be working here at the facility. I have to be there for my family."

Max shocked me by saying, "You know what, Drew? I totally understand, and your family needs you." I thanked him for understanding and we talked about how far he had come.

Max now walked tall, confident, and sure of his surroundings without fear. I told him to remember everything he worked so hard for. We walked to the bench we had sat on so many days before. This day was sad for me and for him as well. I had been the glue holding him together mentally every day that I had worked there.

"Max, now it is up to you to finish what we started here," I told him.

"I will; what a journey this has been."

We walked back to the facility and had our final meeting that day. I took out the papers from the manila folder that we wrote on every time we met and asked, "What is the plan?"

Max expressed that he would continue to work with his treatment team and with The Moving on Program to discharge.

Max and I had our last meeting on my last day working at the facility. I praised Max for all the hard work he had done over the past year. After our meeting was over, I asked if I could give him a hug. He replied, "Yes."

We stood on the sun porch for the last time. As we hugged, I cried. I envisioned Max when I first had met him, the young man who would not leave his room. He took a chance with a case worker who would help him to become the man he is today.

I wiped my tears and said, "Take care of you. Finish what we started. You will have a great life."

He said the same thing he always had, "I hope so, and I will."

I walked away and that was the last time I saw him.

I believe people come into our lives for a reason. I came into Max's to remind him of the person he was before, who he was before his diagnosis with a mental illness, that he still was that person. Now he was on the search for his inner peace and independence. He came into mine to remind me of my own strength and resilience and to show me that my illness did not define me as a person. From Max, I learned that I needed to finish the work I had started with my own recovery and not be ashamed.

Max is now planning on discharging from the facility through The Moving on Program. My hope for him is that he continues to write, take walks, and go back to finish school, and maybe one day be a philosophy professor or a writer. Whatever he chooses in his life, I hope he will be happy and successful. Who knows what the future holds for that young man? I always said to him and his family, "He will have a good life." I believe he will.

— —

I knew I would miss one woman. When I first started working at the facility, Beth warned me about Sally. I asked Beth, "Why are you warning me?"

"Drew, she is going to hate you and then she might warm up to you." I was apprehensive about meeting Sally.

She was five-foot-eight, had short white and grey hair, and was in her late sixties. She wore jeans every day with a brown belt, big brown boots, and she walked with a cane due to a limp. She wore either a long-sleeved t-shirt with a leather jacket, or if it was summer, she would wear a tank top.

Sally had severe Schizophrenia and was tormented by the voices in her head. Every day she would stand in the hallway on the second floor of the facility, talking to herself while looking out the window. I would walk by to do my rounds and at the top of her lungs she would scream at me, "What did you say to me! Am I going to the hospital!"

I would remain calm and say to her, "Sally, I did not say a word to you, and no you are not going to the hospital."

Sally would then glare at me and say, "Okay then."

This conversation happened every day of the week. Sally had a debilitating fear of going to the hospital. Sally had a brother who paid privately for Sally to live in the facility. He also gave her money and cartons of cigarettes that I would hand out to her daily. Sally did not care for her brother whenever he came to the facility for a care plan meeting. She often yelled at him and became agitated.

Before Sally became ill, she was an artist and I was told she worked making post cards, painting the fronts of them. I bought Sally a sketch pad and pencils so she could be creative. Sally had a habit of leaving all her belongings around the facility and if someone touched them, she went ballistic.

When I gave it to her, she looked at me lucidly with a smile on her face and said, "You bought this for me? Thank you so much. That was so sweet of you." She never ended up drawing in the sketchpad, but she seemed to appreciate the gesture.

Sally would have these lucid moments where she was so gentle and kind. One day we were on the elevator, just Sally and me, going to the second floor. Sally said, "Drew, can you believe I am sixty-eight years old, and I have these voices in my head? It is a living hell."

I was shocked at how lucid she was in this moment and struggled to think of what to say. "Sally, I am sorry that you have to go through this every day. It must be so hard for you."

"It is hard. I appreciate that."

I felt sad for the fact she never felt solace in her mind.

In the hottest months of that summer when I was working, I would wear wide-leg gaucho pants with a tight body suit. Sally came to my office one day and I was wearing this. She smiled and said, "You know what you look like today?"

"What do I look like?"

"You look like a wealthy lady who would be at a party at the Botanical Gardens."

Coming from Sally who half the time was screaming at me for thinking I was putting her in the hospital, I was flattered and welcomed the compliment. "Thank you so much, I am going for a New York vibe with my outfit today."

She smiled and mumbled, "You look nice."

Then she walked away from my office.

I wished every day that the voices that tortured her would go away. On my last day, I told Sally I was not going to work there anymore and that I was leaving to spend time with my family. She told me to "take care of my girls." I found out four months after I quit that Sally had passed away. She was having issues with her stomach, which made her ill. When I heard the news I cried, I was so sad she was gone. At the same time, I was crying because now for the first time in who knows how many years she was mentally at peace. I think of her often and I miss her.

CHAPTER 17

THERAPY

The days and weeks after I left my job at the facility, I would walk to the park. I began to take walks every day to mentally heal from the loss of my job, which I so loved. I would go on the same route every day. I would put on my black leggings, tight black tank, and walking shoes.

I always wore my black LA baseball cap with a low ponytail. I would put in my Air Pods and blast music to tune out everything around me. I loved being able to zone out and just have time to myself. As I walked there, I could feel the warm sun on my skin and smell the summer air with the warm breeze. Birds flew above and into the trees where I was walking. I found calm in this routine. It was like a mental reset for my day.

I felt a pit in my stomach that I was no longer helping those people every day who I really felt connected to. It was as if I was grieving the loss of a passion even though I knew it was time to move on. I wondered how I was going to fill that space in my everyday life to make me feel like I was helping others while at the same time feeling fulfilled myself.

When I walked, I would have the reels like a movie in my mind playing back the moments that helped me look inside of my own pain through the pain of others. I would think about the numerous conversations I would have during the day with residents when I was working, listening to the emotional pain some of them were going through. In those moments, I felt what they were feeling. I had those moments in my life of dark depression. I understood how hard it had been for them. I had to figure out what I was going to do to fill my purpose again. Something that would bring me joy and make me feel as if I was doing something I felt passionate about.

These walks helped me reflect on what I was wanting to do next in my life.

As I have grown older, I have realized that when I was growing up, I was always surrounded by so many friends and acquaintances. I have pushed so many people away that were close to me in my life. I have what is called a "push and pull." I so desperately want to let people know me, to get close and have emotional intimate relationships built on love and trust. Then the fear sets in, hence the push. What if they know my secret, that I have a mental illness? Will they look at me differently? Will they treat me another way because of my illness? Or I push because it is hard for me to feel emotionally vulnerable. This is a very hard process for me. I feel if I am vulnerable, I will be hurt like I was hurt in my past.

All I know is that in the past when I have let others know intimate parts of myself emotionally, when I have opened up, people have given me a common response. Their silence and uncertainty of how to respond doesn't necessarily mean they are judging me, but I still feel so much self-doubt and shame about living with a mental illness. In a world full of so many stigmas about mental illness, can you blame me for being so guarded with my own?

The number of people in the United States who have a diagnosable mental health condition is "nearly one in five adults in any given year. There are forty-four million adults in the United States who have a mental illness. The number of adults who have bipolar disorder is 3.3 million."[47]

I am clearly not alone in the fact that so many people suffer with the same diagnosis. I feel that so many people struggle silently due to the shame of having a diagnosis. In my experience talking to people, acquaintances, friends, and other people I know, they are not talking outwardly about their mental health struggles to other people.

Stigmas have so many harmful effects. These include: "feelings of shame, hopelessness and isolation. Reluctance to ask for help or to get treatment. Lack of understanding by family, friends, or others. Fewer opportunities for employment or social interaction. Bullying, physical violence, or harassment."[48]

Some attitudes have grown worse over time: "When in reality, the people with mental illness are the victims of violence, they are 2.5 times more likely to be victims of violence in the general population, a study found that mental illness alone does not increase the chances a person will become violent.

The statistics and the amount of people who are afraid to discuss their mental illness makes me one out of millions who feel the stigma that comes with the judgment of our society regarding mental illness. This in turn makes people struggle with their illness in silence. The family members of the people who have a mental illness feel the need to "keep the secret" that their loved one is ill. They don't know how to cope with the fact that their loved one has a mental illness.

I have found I am living in a constant state of "trauma mind." It is so hard for me to trust, and this makes it sometimes impossible to let others really get to know me. I often wonder if I am good enough. I act on the outside as if I am great. I laugh and have an upbeat personality. I seem to have my shit together, yet I struggle with sadness and self-doubt.

I feel this way because I cannot bring myself to be my authentic self. I beat myself up constantly for not being better emotionally. I am hopeful that I can continue to have more self-acceptance with who I am and feeling more settled with my diagnosis. It is a part of who I am, not all of who I am as a person.

"Dealing with a family member who has a mood disorder or anxiety can require a lot of effort from a family member—at times I can be exhausting. It can be disruptive to the flow of the entire family's routines and patterns, which is stressful over time."⁴⁹

I have had first-hand exposure to how families can be affected by members with severe mental illness. What I have learned from the residents at the facility is that it depends on the people in the family. Many families become estranged from the person in the family with the mental illness. They feel as though no matter what they do or say they cannot win, or they are constantly walking on eggshells. What the family members who are estranged don't realize is that the person plagued with the mental illness must deal with the shame and the abandonment that comes along with that.

So many residents on my caseload would talk about their parents and siblings they no longer spoke to because of their illness. Many of the residents would tell me they felt abandoned and alone because of this. I would always reassure them that they were not alone, that the staff and the other residents in the facility cared for them and so did I. I always hoped this would make them feel better. We know that social support with people with psychosis, for instance by friends and family, is crucial for recovery.

The family members do not understand how difficult it is for the person with the illness to have to deal with the symptoms, which are sometimes not in their control. No matter what medications they are on or how much therapy that person is in, mental illness does not go away. The person can be in recovery, but they will have the illness forever. The symptoms can be managed and the person with the illness can lead a good life. Every day with a mental illness brings new feelings and emotions. Dealing with symptoms is all about managing your emotions and working with your treatment team, therapist, psychiatrist, and your support system. All of these are a huge help in the recovery stages of mental illness.

The families I worked with who were in their daughters', sons', or siblings' lives all had one thing in common, acceptance of what they could not change.

They would say, "I know my (sister, brother, daughter, son) is sick but I choose to accept when it is difficult and not get angry. I choose to support and love them anyway because they did not ask to be sick or ill in their mind."

I was always in awe of these family members because the easiest way to deal with mental illness is to turn the other way. My experience with the families who could not handle their loved one's illness was the lack of education regarding mental illness. In turn, they did not know how to emotionally and empathetically give their loved one the support they so desperately needed.

Now in 2021, the patients have autonomy. Families help but don't necessarily make all their decisions... The individual who is receiving the treatment gets to make their own independent decisions of what is best for them and their treatment plan.

In the 1920s, when families could involuntarily put their loved ones in hospitals and institutions, the decisions were mostly made by another or the family itself. Now the patient has a say in what he or she wants to do with their mental health treatment plans. There must be a release of information from the patient to accept the care needed. Now people with mental illness are treated as people not as incompetent animals that cannot make their own choices for themselves.

The history of treatments on the mentally ill brain is fascinating and traumatizing. A variety of controversial treatments have been used in the past for individuals with mental illnesses.

"Deliberately creating a low blood sugar coma gained attention in the 1930s as a tool for treating mental illness because it was believed that dramatically changing insulin levels altered wiring in the brain. This treatment lasted for several more decades, with many practitioners swearing by the purported positive results for patients who went through this treatment. The comas lasted for one to four hours, and the treatment thankfully faded from use during the 1960s."[50]

As the understanding of mental illness evolved, some practitioners came to believe that seizures from such conditions as epilepsy and mental illness (including schizophrenia) could not exist together.[51]

The doctors purposefully gave the patients seizures, but they then realized later that inducing the seizures did nothing to help the patient's mental illness. Later this led to the more effective study of electric shocks and ECT. "

"The Ancient Greeks had observed that a period of fever sometimes cured people of other symptoms, but it wasn't until the late 1800s that fevers were induced to try to treat mental illness. The psychiatrist would induce syphilis and malaria into patients. They thought that inducing diseases into patients might help cure them. These extreme measures did not help the patient in any way.[52]

Through the therapy I am now involved in I am doing EMDR, which is Eye Movement Desensitization and Reprocessing. This psychotherapy treatment was originally designed to alleviate the distress associated with traumatic memories.53

During Eye Movement Desensitization and Reprocessing the client attends to emotionally disturbing material in brief sequential doses while simultaneously focusing on an external stimulus. This therapy is so intensive, and it literally is retraining your brain. My first session was so intense it took a week for me to come back to baseline with my anxiety and depression. I am going through Eye Movement Desensitization and Reprocessing to get back to who I was before all the abuse in my life changed the chemicals in my brain. I am hopeful, after being in therapy most of my life, that I am ready for new unconventional ways to heal my brain.

"It is an evidence-based practice that has been shown to have an 80 percent success rate with post-traumatic stress disorder. Eye Movement Desensitization and Reprocessing stimulates our brain's natural ability to process life events so that we can let go of the emotional distress connected to our past."54

For me, talk therapy and Eye Movement Desensitization and Reprocessing with the right medication makes me feel more balanced. I am starting to feel a transformation in how I deal with certain emotions and behaviors that I have. I don't feel that I ruminate as much as I had before about certain situations. I would always have a nonstop reel in my mind telling me I was broken or a failure because of my mental illness. Since Eye Movement Desensitization and Reprocessing, I have had more self-acceptance and self-forgiveness than I had before.

This is a slow process, and I am taking it as such. I want to do it the right way this time and not just go through the motions. Without being fully invested into the healing that I must go through, recovery is not guaranteed.

I am very grateful that I was not born in the 1800s, being injected with diseases, or being put into an insulin-induced coma. I, the patient, get to choose what I feel comfortable with in my own treatment, rather than someone like a family member or a doctor making these decisions for me. Now I can choose my treatment plan with the help of my treatment team what works best for my individualized plan.

I am not going to sit here and bullshit you. The past months have been the most trying and painful. I must look inside my feelings of self-hate, guilt, shame, trust issues, sadness, hopelessness, and fear. All these emotions are not new to me; I have had them my whole life. The fact I am facing each one head-on is so frightening. I am ready to do this and am putting the work in one time a week with my therapist. We all have demons we face internally. Few people look those emotions in the eye and say, "Let's see where you came from." She is a kind and gentle woman. She has a nonjudgmental stance and I feel as though she sees me not my illness.

CHAPTER 18

PEACEFUL

———

For me, having a mental illness is exhausting. Let me paint the picture of what a day in my brain looks like. When I wake up in the morning, I open my eyes and wonder, *today will I feel depressed, irritable, moody, bitchy, annoyed, angry for no reason at all?*

Imagine feeling these emotions while having nothing to trigger them. You just feel this way and cannot control it. "Normal" people have something that triggers the emotion of being annoyed, like a child tugging at your shirt while you are on the phone and must get off. This is not the case for me; no one is tugging. I am just fucking annoyed, and for what? No reason whatsoever. The chemicals in my brain make me feel these emotions with no alarm to tell me it's coming.

The people who live with me—Tyler and my girls—see how I am behaving annoyed for no apparent reason. We will be sitting at dinner and Sara will be chewing loudly. I will say to her, "Can you please stop chewing so loudly. It is really annoying." The table will get awkward and tense.

Sara says, "Mom, that hurt my feelings. Why are you being so rude?"

Then the shame sets in of why I cannot control these emotions. *Why do I let the emotions I feel take over me?* I know rationally that Sara is just chewing, not to annoy me but as a function of eating her food. Then the embarrassment sets in and says, *Drew, why are you showing your kids this emotion? You are a bad mother for not controlling it.* The reel in my brain of good and bad emotions goes on all day long.

Sometimes when I open my eyes in the morning, I wonder if I will go the other way and feel softer, more vulnerable, playful, patient, talkative, in a good mood, and happy. Tyler, Madison, and Sara are on a mood roller coaster every day not knowing which up or down they will get. I truly feel for them because it is not easy on the other side.

I feel sick inside knowing that I can't just have a "normal" brain. *Why did I get this brain of insanity? Oh, I remember. My abusive father!* I think often if I did not have the verbal and physical abuse I endured, would the chemicals in my brain have been the same?

"Children who suffer from child traumatic stress are those who have been exposed to one or more traumas over the course of their lives and develop reactions that persist and affect their daily lives after the events have ended."[55] Knowing what the research says, I understand there are reasons why my brain is wired this way. It does not make it any easier to live with every day.

My children are teenagers, and they observe me and how I behave. As parents, we hope we are doing our best raising our kids. I think a lot about how my mental illness is affecting them. I asked my youngest daughter Sara one day, "Sara, do you think I am a good mom? What can I do to be better?"

Sara looked at me with a puzzled look on her face. "Mom, you are a great mom. You are always there for Madison and me."

So, then I think, *well, maybe you are doing a good job and they don't see your illness. They just see you as their mom.* I worry about whether my daughters will struggle with their own worries about their mental health once they learn what their mother has been facing. I have not yet told Madison and Sara that I have Bipolar.

Everyone chooses when to tell their children about their illness and I am not ready to discuss this with mine. Honestly, I am still coming to terms with my diagnosis. How can I make them understand when I am still trying to understand myself? One day they will read this book and maybe it will help them understand how my illness came about. Then we can have a conversation if they have any questions for me and I can support them in the process of understanding me and the diagnosis.

I also do not want them to use this diagnosis toward me in conversation if they are upset. Teenagers can be difficult and not quite understand the ins and outs of mental illness. Their brains are still developing. I want them to just see me as their mother, not their "bipolar mother."

There is no guidebook for having a mental illness and having children. I do know I am a good mother and will continue being one. "Parental mental illness doesn't have to be a negative force in a child's life and having a mental health disorder doesn't mean you are a bad parent.

It does, however, mean you need support to overcome your psychological struggles and nurture your relationships with your children."[56] No one is perfect, mental illness or not. I live for my girls and will always be supportive and love them with all of me.

From the time I was a small child, being around water has made me feel peaceful. The definition of peaceful is "Freedom from disturbance; quiet and tranquility."[57] When I am around water, such as a lake or an ocean, this is exactly how water has made me feel.

I walk every day to clear my mind, and I enjoy going to the lake near my house to watch and listen to the waves hitting the shore. "Research finds that spending time by the ocean or a body of water is good for your wellbeing. An English census date published in the journal Health Place, those who live by the coast report better physical and mental health than those who don't."[58]

From the time I was a young girl, I have always had a dream that when I grew older, I would buy a place right on the ocean. I still hope to someday buy a home by the ocean. I pictured Aruba or the Maldives, the water turquoise blue and when you look down you can see the fish swimming beneath your feet. I pictured a small house with a thatched roof and two bedrooms, the house would have a big open living space with the windows open to let the island breeze go through the house.

When Tyler, the girls, and I have traveled to Aruba, Florida, or Mexico in the morning and at sunset, I would walk on the beach alone and take in the air, sun, breeze, the calm, and the ocean sounds. The only time I have not felt anxiety, or any symptoms from my illness, is when I am near a body of water. I have never shared this with anyone in my life, not even my own husband. I think maybe because this is something I just hold sacred to me.

I have met another who feels this way around water and about their illness. When I was working at the facility a resident I worked with said the same thing about how water affected him, that when he was around water, he also felt at peace within his mind the same as I had. I had not shared with this resident that I felt the same around water.

I think that the goal of my recovery is to get to the peaceful place that water brings me to. "Recovery from mental disorders is a process of change through which individuals: Improve their health and wellness, live a self-directed life, and strive to achieve their full potential."[59] I want all these things, and I know they are possible for me.

I use my healthy coping skills that I have learned through Dialectical Behavioral Therapy. When I look at specific situations that I have a hard time dealing with, I realize I can change my emotions by how I am thinking. Then my behaviors and reactions begin to change. This might seem like a simple task, but for me this is very difficult. I must use my recovery plan that I have made for myself with my treatment team.

I identify the goals I must achieve for my mental wellness. I specifically map out what I can do to reach these goals daily and throughout my week. I track any mental health issues I am having, any change in my behaviors and moods. I identify the triggers that make me feel stressed and bring out my symptoms of my bipolar. All these goals I set for my mental health to heal is my recovery journey.

The Eye Movement Desensitization and Reprocessing therapy is also helpful in my ongoing recovery. It takes me out of the trauma mind that prevents me from having vulnerability and openness with others. The therapy helps me in the healing process and makes me feel more balanced in my days, rather than feeling constantly anxious and ruminating about past events in my childhood.

Recovery is a journey, and it has not been an easy one. I am still in recovery and am trying to find a balance of self-acceptance, sitting with the fact just because I have a mental illness it does not define me. It is a part of who I am. Some days are so difficult I feel like I don't want to face the world and get out of bed. Then I think, *Drew, you have come so far. Get up and make this day better than the last.* Giving up for me is not an option.

CHAPTER 19

SELF-REALIZATION

Self-realization is the fulfillment of one's own potential.[60] With intensive therapy, being on the right medication, and having connections and support from others that I feel safe and comfortable with, I often wonder, *Am I on my way to my own self-realization?*

I used to feel that I was broken and damaged, that having Bipolar two Disorder made me unlovable. I felt if I did not hide this part of who I was from others, the "secret" would get out. Then I would be stigmatized and talked about in the community I live in. I also feared the people I have grown up with knowing that I have a mental illness, worrying that they would talk and gossip about me behind my back to others. Let's be honest, that is not too far-fetched. How many people have been gossiped about even without having a mental illness? I don't usually care what others think about me, but when it comes to the vulnerability of others knowing my struggles with my mental health, I feel emotionally naked.

This is a real fear of mine, and I have to really try to take my own advice that I gave to a resident from the facility I worked at: "When you stop leading with your illness and come to terms with the fact you have this illness, things begin to heal, to shift and then the recovery really starts to happen. The shame of having your illness begins to fade with time."

Throughout this book, I have been vulnerable and honest about my life journey, but I still have so many friends who do not know about my diagnosis. At times in my life the mask has come off. One time stands out when I was so emotionally vulnerable with two of my girlfriends that it was a sort of "freak out" moment for me. I went on a trip to Aruba with two women I was becoming close friends with. The whole day at the pool we drank margaritas; I must have had five total throughout the day. Anyone who really knows me realizes this is a lot of alcohol for me to consume. I am a "light weight" when it comes to drinking.

When we got back to the hotel room it was about 4 p.m. and we all decided to get dressed to go out to dinner. When we got to the restaurant one my friends said, "Hey, I have a pot pen. How about we smoke?"

I am not big on smoking pot, and I have never done any drugs because addiction runs in my family. But I thought, *Why the hell not? I am on vacation.*

I took two puffs of the pen and after a half hour I felt very high and emotional. I felt it coming, me starting to open about my past, which I was not planning on sharing on this trip. With tears in my eyes, I began to talk about my father, sharing pieces of stories about the abuse that I had gone through. I was mortified that they would find out my "secret" of me not being emotionally okay at times.

To my surprise, one friend said, "Drew, it is okay. I am so sorry you had to go through those things growing up."

"Thanks. It is okay."

I forced myself to smile and change the subject quickly before I divulged any other of my secrets. Inside I was screaming at myself for not being able in that moment to be an actress and keep my shit together. I gave myself room for forgiveness because I knew that sometimes I had to be vulnerable. I am only human.

The next day, what I shared was not discussed and for that I was grateful. What was strange to me is that it brought us closer in a way. Many months later my friend thanked me for being vulnerable and sharing part of my story. She said to me, "Everyone goes through things with their families, and you had the strength that night to share part of your story."

What this taught me was to be more trusting about being vulnerable in a safe space.

Not everyone is going to be judgmental when it comes to being open with my feelings. I can count the number of close friends I have on one hand, but it is not about quantity; it is about the quality of the ones you choose to have in your life. Now instead of wearing a mask of shame, so to speak about my illness, I am becoming more at peace with accepting my illness as part of my recovery journey. I don't want to live my whole life hating myself for something that is not my fault.

The road to recovery, to self-realization, and fulfilling my own life's potential is a challenging one. Having a mental illness is not like having a broken arm. A broken arm heals and goes back to regular function in time. A mental illness is lifelong and does not ever fully heal. It is always present in some way. But with the right psychological therapies and medication, recovery can happen quicker and the risk of relapse decreases.

Being emotionally vulnerable is very hard for me, but I know in order to continue the path to my own self-realization, I must accept the things I cannot change. I cannot change the past, but I can change the outcome of my future. I am in control of my emotions and behaviors. I choose to be fully present in my own life. I will continue working on being emotionally healthy as I move forward.

I am taking all the right steps with my recovery. I have a treatment team with a wonderful therapist I see one time a week. I also have a great psychiatrist who makes sure I am taking the right medication in the right dosage to keep my ups and downs controlled. I use healthy coping skills such as exercise, going on walks daily, calling friends and family to connect, and being present in my relationships. I am present for Tyler and the girls, and I spend time with them and connect with them on many different emotional levels.

These support systems and my willingness to use the skills I have learned are essential to my recovery. When I was at my worst with my illness, I never used healthy coping skills. I always avoided connection and emotional intimacy because that was the easy way out. Recovery is work and it is very hard every day, but I am choosing to try and live my best life. I deserve it. Having this illness is a day-to-day process, and some days I do not feel like connecting, and I retreat within myself emotionally. Recovery is all about the work you put in. I do try my best every day to be self-aware of how I am feeling.

I am realizing I don't always have to have a mask on. Sometimes I can take it off and show others who I really am. Having a mental illness your whole life is not easy, but what you do with it really makes the difference. For me, I looked internally and asked, *Am I going to sit in self-pity? Or am I going to do the work to change my outlook on myself and my life with this illness?*

I was having a conversation with a close friend, Blake. She always has such wonderful insight into how I can deal with my pain inside. She said, "You have to move forward in your life."

She is right. I have lived for so long blaming myself for my mental pain when it is time to let it go. Let go of the self-hate and start to have more self-acceptance and self-love.

I also have managed throughout these years to not be hospitalized for having thoughts of suicide or self-harm. I look at those thoughts and feelings as a darkness inside of a person and the person must pull through that darkness to come out of the other end alive and well.

I chose to reach out to my family and Tyler for the support I needed when I was going through those difficult times. I was put on the right medicine and went into intensive therapy to deal with the darkness of those feelings I had to work through.

What I have learned from navigating through this darkness is that there is always another day to live and always a light that follows the darkness. Life is too precious to live out of the pain in the moment, and suicide is never an option. I am so forever grateful that I used my sound mind and healthy coping skills in those moments. I have had so many wonderful things happen to me because I chose to live. What I have discovered in sharing my story is that my life has been one of survival and resilience. I am living and breathing proof it does get better.

Suicide and self-harm are never the answer to getting through the darkness. At the time a person might feel this is the only option, but the only real option is to work through the pain. Many people who experience similar thoughts and feelings do not discuss them, or if they do, not often enough.

But you are not alone. If you are struggling with thoughts of suicide or self-harm, reach out for help. The National Suicide Prevention Lifeline is always available at 1-800-273-8255. There is also an online chat suicidepreventionlifeline.org[61] This could help save your life, and your life is so worth saving.

Nothing is harder than having a diagnosis and feeling like you can't articulate what you are going through. Unless a person has experienced something, it is very hard for them to understand what the other person is going through. I choose to share my story so others who know someone with a mental illness can have a better understanding of what mental illness is and what the person who has the illness must deal with daily. I am hopeful this will help them be more empathetic when a loved one or friend experiences the symptoms of a mental illness.

By writing this book I am coming into my own self-realization, meaning I am finally seeing myself as a healthy functioning person in the world. I cannot change what happened to me as child, but I can use my experiences to help others. If I never had gone through what I had as a child, I would have never written this book. I am looking forward to being able to use this book as a conversation starter to help educate people so the stigma of mental illness can be lifted.

The world needs more understanding, compassion, and peace when it comes to people's hearts and minds. Let my story inspire you to reach out to the people in your life struggling silently. If you yourself are struggling silently, know that you are not alone. Healing is a process, but I am living proof it gets better with time. My journey is not over yet, and I have many more memories to make.

If you ever have thoughts of suicide or self-harm you are not alone. The National Suicide Prevention Lifeline provides twenty-four-seven support. The number to call is 1-800-273-8255. Another helpful resource is the crisis text line. A crisis counselor for self-harm can be reached at 741741 or you can use the mobile click to text button on crisistextline.org. Another resource for help when battling thoughts of self-harm number is 1-800-448-3000 or www.yourlifeyourvoice. org/email: Text VOICE to 20121

APPENDIX

CHAPTER 2

Keim, Brandon. "How Abuse Changes a Child's Brain." *Wired.* December 5, 2011. https://www.wired.com/2011/12/neurology-of-abuse/.

Meyers, McKenna. "Fatherless Daughters: How Growing Up Without a Dad Affects Women." *We Have Kids.* February 28, 2020. https://wehavekids.com/family-relationships/When-Daddy-Dont-Love-Their-Daughters-What-Happens-to-Women-Whose-Fathers-Werent-There-for-Them

Morin, Amy LCSW. "What is Emotional Child Abuse?" Medically reviewed by Steven Gans, MD. Updated March 8, 2021. http://www.verywellfamily.com/what-is-emotional-child-abuse-4157502.

University College London. "Maltreated Children Show Same Pattern of Brain Activity as Combat Soldiers." *ScienceDaily.* May 13, 2021. http://www.sciencedaily.com/releases/2011/12/111205140406.htm.

US Department of Health and Human Services, Children's Bureau. "Understanding the Effects of Maltreatment on Brain Development." (Washington, DC, 2015) https://www.childwelfare.gov/pubPDFs/brain_development.pdf.

CHAPTER 3

Weiss, Robert. PhD, MSW. "Emotional Incest: How to Recognize This Form of Covert Sexual Abuse." *MBG Health*. Last updated February 28, 2020. https://www.mindbodygreen.com/0-23980/the-insidious-type-of-sexual-abuse-you-might-be-ignoring.html

CHAPTER 4

Holland, Kimberly, "Bipolar Disorder and Anger: Why It Happens and How to Cope." Medically reviewed by Steven Gans, MD. Last Updated January 31, 2021. https://www.healthline.com/health/bipolar-disorder/bipolar-anger

Merriam-Webster. s.v. (n) "Disassociation." Accessed May 13, 2021. https://www.merriam-webster.com/dictionary/disassociation

Smith, Melinda, M.A., and Jeanne Segal, PhD. "Bipolar Disorder Signs and Symptoms." *Help Guide*. Last Updated September 2020. https://www.helpguide.org/articles/bipolar-disorder/bipolar-disorder-signs-and-symptoms.htm

Smith, Melinda, M.A., Lawrence Robinson, and Jeanne Segal, PhD. "Depression Symptoms and Warning Signs." *Help Guide*. Last updated April 2021. https://www.helpguide.org/articles/depression/depression-symptoms-and-warning-signs.htm

WebMD. "What is Dissociation?" Reviewed by Joseph Goldberg, MD. August 26, 2019. https://www.webmd.com/mental-health/dissociation-overview

CHAPTER 5

WebMD. "Types of Bipolar Disorder." Reviewed by Jennifer Casarella, MD. Last Updated April 20, 2021. https://www.webmd.com/bipolar-disorder/guide/bipolar-disorder-forms

CHAPTER 6

Crisis Text Line. 2013-2021. https://www.crisistextline.org

Mayo Clinic. "Depression (Major depressive disorder)." https://www.mayoclinic.org/diseases-conditions/depression/symptoms-causes/syc-20356007

The National Suicide Prevention Lifeline. Accessed May 13, 2021. https://suicidepreventionlifeline.org

Your Life Your Voice. Accessed May 13, 2021. https://www.yourlifeyourvoice.org/Pages/home.aspx

CHAPTER 8

Postpartum Depression. "What Is Postpartum Depression?" Accessed May 14, 2021. https://www.postpartumdepression.org

CHAPTER 9

Dietz, Lisa. "DBT Self Help." (2001-2018). https://www.dbtselfhelp.com

Drugs.com. IBM Watson Micromedex. "Depakote." Multum, Cerner. Updated May 4, 2021. https://www.drugs.com/search.php?searchterm=Depakote&a=1

Drugs.com. IBM Watson Micromedex. "Lamictal." Multum, Cerner. Updated May 4, 2021. https://www.drugs.com/search. php?searchterm=Lamictal&a=1

Drugs.com. IBM Watson Micromedex. "Lexapro." Multum, Cerner. Updated May 4, 2021.https://www.drugs.com/search. php?searchterm=Lexapro&a=1

Drugs.com. IBM Watson Micromedex. "Topamax." Multum, Cerner. Updated May 4, 2021. https://www.drugs.com/search. php?searchterm=Topamax&a=1

Drugs.com. IBM Watson Micromedex. "Trileptal." Multum, Cerner. Updated May 4, 2021. https://www.drugs.com/search. php?searchterm=Trileptal&a=1

Drugs.com. IBM Watson Micromedex. "Zyprexa." Multum, Cerner. Updated May 4, 2021. https://www.drugs.com/search. php?searchterm=Zyprexa&a=1

CHAPTER 13

Mayo Clinic. "Obsessive-Compulsive Disorder (OCD)." Accessed May 14, 2021. https://www.mayoclinic.org/diseases-conditions/ obsessive-compulsive-disorder/symptoms-causes/syc-20354432

National Center for Victims of Crime. "Child Sexual Abuse Statistics." Accessed May 14, 2021. https://victimsofcrime.org/ child-sexual-abuse-statistics/

Ottisova, Livia, Patrick Smith, Hitesh Shetty, Daniel Stahl, Jonny Downs, and Sian Oram. "Psychological Consequences of Child Trafficking: A Historical Cohort Study of Trafficked Children in Contact with Secondary Mental Health Services." Published March 8, 2018. https://www.ncbi.nlm.nih.gov/pmc/articles/PMC5843209/

CHAPTER 14

Harvard Health Publishing Harvard Medical School. "If You've Been Exposed to the Coronavirus." 2021. https://www.health.harvard.edu/diseases-and-conditions/if-youve-been-exposed-to-the-coronavirus

Rush University Medical Center. "Rush Preparing for Covid-19 Resurgence." *News Wise.* October 27, 2020. https://www.newswise.com/coronavirus/rush-preparing-for-covid-19-resurgence

CHAPTER 15

Frye, Devon. "Mental Illness Splits Families: How to Avoid Losing Your Family." May 18, 2017. https://www.psychologytoday.com/us/blog/view-the-mist/201705/mental-illness-splits-families

Jiang, Jeannette, Emily Peterson, and Robert Heimer. "Covid-19 Updated Data and Developments—March 23, 2020." March 23, 2020. https://publichealth.yale.edu/news-article/23317/

Mayo Clinic. "Mental health: Overcoming the Stigma of Mental Illness." Mayo Clinic Staff, 1998–2021. https://www.mayoclinic.org/diseases-conditions/mental-illness/in-depth/mental-health/art-20046477

National Institute of Mental Health. "Statistics." https://www.nimh.nih.gov/health/statistics/?__hst-c=223762052.7ac90759547c82c8ff9f2acca6c9b

f6b.1366571304664.1366571304664.1366571304664.1&__
hssc=223762052.1.1366571304664

CHAPTER 16

Leonhardt, Megan. "9.8 million Working Mothers in the US Suffering from Burnout." *CNBC*. Published December 3, 2020. https://www.cnbc.com/2020/12/03/millions-of-working-mothers-in-the-us-are-suffering-from-burnout.html

Beidas, Marcus, Courtney Benjamin Powell, Byron Wolk, Arthur Evans, Gregory Aarons, Matthew Hadery, Trevor Huford, Lucia Walsh, Danielle Adams, Frances Barg, Shaili Babbar, and David Mandell. National Center for Biotechnology Information. "A Prospective Examination of Clinician and Supervisor Turnover Within the Context of Implementation of Evidence-Based Practices in a Publicly-Funded Mental Health System." National Library of Medicine. September 2016. https://pubmed.ncbi.nlm.nih.gov/26179469/

CHAPTER 17

Frye, Devon. "Mental Illness Splits Families: How to Avoid Losing Your Family." *Psychology Today*. May 18, 2017. https://www.psychologytoday.com/us/blog/view-the-mist/201705/mental-illness-splits-families

Mental Health America. "Bipolar Disorder." 2021. https://www.mhanational.org/conditions/bipolar-disorder

Mental Health America. "Quick Facts and Statistics about Mental Health." 2021. https://www.mhanational.org/mentalhealthfacts

Osborne, Sarah, LPC, LADC, MATS. "The Power of EMDR." October 4, 2017. https://mountainside.com/blog/addiction-treatment/the-power-of-emdr/

Shapiro, Francine. "EMDR, Adaptive Information Processing, and Case Conceptualization. 2017. https://connect.springerpub.com/content/sgremdr/1/2/68

Vann, Madeline R., MPH. "The 10 Worst Mental Health Treatments in History." Medically reviewed by Lindsey Marcellin, MD, MPH. *Everyday Health.* Updated May 7, 2014. https://www.everydayhealth.com/pictures/worst-mental-health-treatments-history/

CHAPTER 18

BBC News. "People Feel Healthier on the English Coast." July 17, 2012. https://www.bbc.com/news/health-18856680

Kvarnstrom, Elisabet. "The Effects of Parental Mental Illness on Children and the Need for Healing." *Mountainside.* April 14, 2016. https://www.bridgestorecovery.com/blog/the-effects-of-parental-mental-illness-on-children-and-the-need-for-healing/

CHAPTER 19

MentalHealth.gov. "Recovery Is Possible." Updated 2021. https://www.mentalhealth.gov/.basics/recovery-possible

National Suicide Prevention Lifeline. Accessed May 14, 2021. https://suicidepreventionlifeline.org

Your Life Your Voice. Accessed May 13, 2021. https://www.yourlifeyourvoice.org/Pages/home.aspx

ENDNOTES

---

1   Merriam-Webster, 2021
2   University College London, 2011
3   Keim, 2011
4   Healy, 2004
5   Morin, 2021
6   McKenna Myers, 2020
7   Weiss, 2020
8   Weiss, 2020
9   Weiss, 2020
10 Merriam-Webster, 1828
11 Goldberg, 2019
12 Smith, Robinson, Seigal, 2021
13 Smith, Segal, 2020
14 Smith, Segal, 2020
15 Smith, Segal, 2020
16 Holland, 2021
17 Casarella, 2021
18 Casarella, 2021
19 Casarella, 2021
20 mayoclinic.org, 2021
21 Crisis Text Line, 2021

22 postpartumdepression.org, 2021

23 postpartumdepression.org, 2021

24 Dietz, 2018

25 Dietz, 2018

26 Watson, 2021

27 Watson, 2021

28 Watson, 2021

29 Watson, 2021

30 Watson, 2021

31 Watson, 2021

32 National Center for Victims of Crime, 2021

33 National Center for Victims of Crime, 2021

34 Ottisova, 2018

35 Mayo Clinic, 2021

36 Rush University Medical Center, 2020

37 Harvard Medical School, 2020

38 Jiang, Peterson, Heimer, 2020

39 Jiang, Peterson, Heimer, 2020

40 Merriam-Webster Dictionary 1828

41 Mayo Clinic, 2021

42 National Institute of Mental Health, 2021

43 Frye, 2017

44 Beidas. 2001

45 National Center for Biotechnology Information, 2016

46 Leonhardt, 2020

47 Mental Health America, 2021

48 Mayo Clinic, 2021

49 Frye, 2017

50 Vann, 2014

51 Vann, 2014

52 Vann, 2014

53 Shapiro, 1989a 1989b

54 Osborne, 2017
55 The National Child Traumatic Stress Network
56 Kvarnstrom, 2016
57 New Oxford American Dictionary
58 BBC News, 2012
59 MentalHealth.gov, 2019
60 New Oxford American Dictionary
61 National Suicide Prevention, 2021